FRUGILLIONAIRE

FRUGILLIONAIRE

500 Fabulous Ways
To Live Richly
And
Save A Fortune

FRANCINE JAY

ANJA PRESS
MEDFORD NJ

Frugillionaire: 500 Fabulous Ways to Live Richly and Save a Fortune

Cover photo: iStockphoto.com

ISBN 10: 0-9840873-0-3
ISBN 13: 978-0-9840873-0-3
Library of Congress Control Number: 2009905473

Printed in the United States of America

Contents

Introduction

Are you frustrated with your finances? Drowning in debt? Or just wondering where your money goes each month? You're not alone! After the mortgage, car loan, taxes, telephone, fuel, electricity and water bills, there's often little left over in the family budget.

Yet ads everywhere beckon us to buy nicer houses, newer cars, hotter gadgets, hipper clothes, better furniture, bigger televisions, fancier housewares and finer foods. That's a lot of pressure on your paycheck! Must you be a millionaire just to make ends meet?

Not if you read this book! For herein lies the secret to financial peace and harmony: how to become a frugillionaire.

Unlike millionaires and billionaires, frugillionaires aren't defined by the number of zeroes in their net worth, or the haute couture in their closets. They don't have personal assistants or private planes. They don't summer in the Hamptons, winter in the islands, or fly to Paris for the weekend.

Quite the contrary: frugillionaires master the art of frugality—living richly while saving a fortune. They make the most of the money they have, and treasure those things that money can't buy. Though they're adept at cutting costs, their lives are not about deprivation. In fact, the appreciation with which they approach each day brings them wealth beyond measure.

And the best part? Becoming a frugillionaire is easier than you think! You don't need to work 24/7, hit the lottery, or hope for a big inheritance. And it certainly doesn't involve any risky investments or get-rich-quick schemes.

All it takes is a new perspective and a few good habits. It's not a quick fix diet, where you starve your desire to shop—only to indulge later in a massive spending binge! Nor do you have to pinch pennies as tediously as you would count calories. It's more like adopting a Mediterranean diet: making wise choices that gradually add up to a genuine lifestyle change.

Becoming a frugillionaire is like slimming down your figure—or in this case, fattening up your bank account—without ever feeling unsatisfied. You'll savor life with new gusto, while saving more money than you ever imagined!

Sounds pretty great, doesn't it? But how on earth do you do it?

When you set out to save money, it's hard to know where to start. You may have the best of intentions, but lack the techniques. Well, this book gives you five hundred of them— all foolproof and fabulous! You won't find sermons about reusing baggies or buying day old bread; the focus here is on fun. These tips show you how to slash expenses, while enjoying the experience.

We'll start off in Chapter 1 with a subject we all love: food! We'll discuss how to dine on a dime, while still enjoying delicious, nutritious (even gourmet!) meals. The cost-cutting techniques cover everything from cooking at home, to hitting the town for dinner and cocktails. From picnics to potlucks, you'll learn creative ways to pare expenses—while maximizing your eating pleasure!

We'll also explore how to save at the supermarket, including why you should bring your coupons and calculator—but not your kids—to the store. And you'll see how a few simple changes in your eating habits can save you thousands of dollars each year!

Chapters 2 and 3 are devoted to housing. It's one of our biggest expenses, and therefore a golden opportunity for saving! You'll learn how to cut your heating and cooling costs, pull the plug on energy leaks, and lower your water bills. We'll also cover how to save on insurance, and get the best value from phone and internet plans.

Then we'll have some fun decorating our abodes, and see how frugillionaires make their homes their castles—without king-size budgets! The design techniques, DIY projects and housecleaning tips detailed here provide all the know-how you need to create a stylish home on a shoestring.

We'll go outdoors in Chapter 4, and learn how to grow beautiful gardens without spending a lot of green. You'll get great advice on composting, conserving water, and choosing and cultivating plants (including how to get them for free!). Put these tips into practice for a lush landscape that's low-maintenance and low-cost.

In Chapter 5, it's our turn for a makeover! Frugillionaires are anything but frumpy: find out how they dress to the nines on next to nothing, and always manage to stay in style. You'll learn how to invest in versatile pieces that are right for you, your figure, and your lifestyle—and build a fashionable wardrobe without spending a fortune.

Chapter 6 helps you get the most bang for your beauty buck. Don't spend another dime on miracle creams until you've read through this section. You'll get great ideas for luxurious, DIY spa treatments, and learn how products like olive oil and baking soda can help you stay beautiful on a budget. We'll also detail some free, all-natural ways to improve your appearance and health—so you'll be gorgeous *and* rich!

We'll break for some frugillionaire-style entertainment in Chapters 7 and 8. Don't worry, there's no karaoke involved—just some fun-loving tips for soaking up some culture, getting your groove on, and otherwise having a blast without breaking the bank.

Whether you're an art lover, movie buff, or music fan, you'll find savvy techniques to get your fix on the cheap. This section also offers a treasure trove of ideas for free, and low-cost, recreational activities. You'll be amazed at how many wonderful ways you can entertain your guests, your kids and yourself—with little need for your wallet.

Transportation—and how to save when you're on the move—is the topic of Chapter 9. Included are gas-saving tips to cut the cost of your commute, as well as some valuable advice on selecting, maintaining and insuring your automobile. We'll also explore alternative methods of transit—and the possibility of eliminating your fuel (and car) expenses entirely!

Chapter 10 shows you how to travel the world without a trust fund. It has tons of tips for tourists on a budget: from scoring the best deals on flights and hotel rooms, to saving on dining, transit and sightseeing costs. You'll learn how frugillionaires live like locals while on vacation—spending less, and enjoying a richer, more authentic, experience.

Chapter 11 isn't about declaring bankruptcy—but how to avoid it! This section is a fitness program for your finances. Tips on shopping, banking and investing will help you hone your money skills and pump up your savings. You'll learn how to track expenditures, use credit wisely, and grow your net worth. Heed the advice herein, and you'll be on the fast track to early retirement.

If you have children (or plans for them), then Chapter 12 is required reading. It gives you all the tips you need to raise happy kids on a pint-sized budget. From outfitting a nursery for a new arrival, to dealing with day care, diapers and dance lessons, you'll find plenty of low-cost ways to nurture your little ones. And with any luck, they'll grow up to follow in your frugillionaire footsteps!

In Chapter 13, we'll deck the halls, without going into debt. By reining in costs, and giving thrifty (yet thoughtful) gifts, you'll avoid a financial hangover come January. But more importantly, you'll capture the true spirit of the holiday season—by spending time with friends and family, rather than spending money.

We'll finish up in Chapter 14 with some frugillionaire philosophy. These last twenty tidbits are the foundation of our frugal, yet fabulous, lifestyle. Why save them for the grand finale? So they'll stay fresh in your mind as you set forth on your path to prosperity!

Ready to get started? Five hundred techniques for saving a fortune are at your fingertips! Pick and choose them, slice and dice them, mix and match them into your own personal formula for financial success.

Though they're organized into categories, there's no need to follow the sequence. Read the book forwards, backwards, upside down, one tip a day, or all at once. Feel free to skip around to your heart's content.

But above all, don't delay: you won't get any richer until you turn the page!

Chapter 1

FOOD

Dining on a Dime, and Saving at the Supermarket

---

1 Put on your chef's hat

Fatten up your wallet with some good, old-fashioned home cooking! At the average restaurant, you'll spend about $20 per person to cover entrées, beverages and tip. Add starters, alcohol and dessert, and the bill rises quickly. In contrast, you could make a delicious dinner (for the whole family!) for less than the cost of an appetizer. If you're not quite at home in the kitchen, get a basic cookbook to learn the fundamentals. Start with the simplest recipes, and tackle more complex dishes as your confidence grows. Enjoy experimenting, and don't worry about perfection; as long as your meal is edible, consider it a success!

2 Cook for an army

We know home cooking is healthy and cheap; but some nights we don't have the time, or energy, to start from scratch. The solution: prepare meals in large batches, and freeze for the week. Batch cooking consolidates your prep work and cleanup into one session, saving precious time on busy evenings. You'll also save money by purchasing ingredients in bulk. If you're really ambitious, cook a month's worth of meals at once; you'll find plenty of recipes on websites, and in cookbooks, devoted to the topic. With ready-to-heat food waiting in the freezer, you'll be much less tempted to splurge on take-out.

3 Love those leftovers

Don't despair when your family leaves food on their plates; be thankful you'll have less cooking to do tomorrow! Frugillionaires know that last night's dinner is the closest thing to a free lunch. Brown bag it the next day, or freeze and serve as a side dish later in the week. By the same token, don't be shy about asking for a doggie bag at a restaurant. Have leftovers wrapped up to go, and get extra mileage from your dining-out dollars. Just be sure to label the containers in the freezer; you'll be reluctant to eat what you can't identify!

4 Eat less meat

Slash your grocery bill by eating less meat! Instead, try less-expensive, protein-rich alternatives like tofu, eggs and fish. For a healthy, well-balanced diet, supplement with fruits and vegetables; whole grains like oatmeal, barley and brown rice; and nuts and legumes like beans, lentils and chickpeas. Reducing your meat consumption has important health, as well as financial, benefits. A less carnivorous lifestyle is associated with lower fat intake and cholesterol levels, and may reduce the risk of heart disease and certain types of cancer—meaning significant savings in future medical costs!

5 Savor seasonal produce

If you buy tomatoes in January, you'll pay dearly for them to be shipped around the globe. Purchase fruits and vegetables in season instead; they're cheaper, fresher, and so much tastier! Nothing's more delicious than corn, blueberries and watermelon in summer; apples, squash and pumpkin in fall; oranges, chestnuts and turnips in winter; and spinach, snow peas and strawberries in spring. Eating seasonally is not just frugal, but joyous. It's a wonderful way to celebrate nature's bounty, and gives us something to look forward to all year round!

6 Get friendly with the farmers

Save money on fruit and vegetables by shopping at the farmers' market. Since the produce is grown locally, transportation costs are low; and with no middlemen to mark up prices, you'll pay much less than you would at the grocery store. What's more, the quality of the food is top-notch, and the ambience sure beats that of a supermarket! Join a CSA (Community Supported Agriculture) program for a steady supply of farm-fresh fare. For a fixed price, you'll receive a weekly basket of produce and other goods—like organic milk, eggs, cheese, herbs and honey. It's a terrific value, and a wonderful experience!

7 Grow your own veggies

Avoid paying for produce altogether, by planting a vegetable garden! Imagine how wonderful it would be to pick fresh lettuce, tomatoes, eggplants or peppers for the evening's dinner—all from your own backyard! You don't need acres of farmland to get started; a small patch of soil, or a few containers, will do. Seeds and starters are inexpensive, and can provide a bountiful harvest for your kitchen table. Peruse books and websites on vegetable gardening to learn how to cultivate and care for your plants. Or hang out at your local farmers' market, chat up the vendors, and get specific tips for your region and climate.

8 Eat breakfast at home

Fried egg sandwiches and jelly donuts are hard on your wallet—and your health! Skip the fast food, but don't skip breakfast. Instead, wake up twenty minutes earlier, and eat it at home. Studies show that people who eat a healthy breakfast consume less fat and cholesterol over the course of the day. They're also better able to control their weight—which can lower healthcare costs down the road. While you're in the kitchen, make your own coffee as well; use a travel mug if you prefer to drink it on-the-go. This simple habit can save hundreds of dollars each year!

9 Cut down on convenience foods

Processed foods save preparation and cooking time, but give you very little bang for your nutritional buck. They're pricey, and often full of sodium, preservatives and saturated fats. However, it's not always practical to cook *everything* from scratch. Therefore, it's best to be strategic with convenience foods: use frozen vegetables when fresh is out of season, or canned stocks and sauces when you don't have time to make your own. But don't buy flavored noodles, microwaveable dinners, and prepackaged peanut butter and jelly sandwiches; these items are just as easy—and certainly more economical—to prepare yourself.

10 Pass on prepackaged servings

Those 100-calorie snack packs are cute—but they're not a good value! In terms of unit price, small, prepackaged servings are often significantly more expensive than "normal" sizes. It can cost double the price (or more!) to have your cookies, crackers or trail mix divvied up for you. Why pay a premium when you can do it yourself? If you have problems with portion control, buy the full-size pack and divide it into ziplock bags or plastic containers. That way, you can enjoy the convenience of a pre-measured amount— without the extra cost!

11 Forget the "instant" food

Instead of instant oatmeal and minute rice, buy bulk oats and uncooked rice. They're significantly cheaper, and much more nutritious! Old-fashioned rolled oats cook in minutes on the stovetop, or in the microwave; add flavor with brown sugar, cinnamon, raisins or dried fruit. You'll not only save money, you'll avoid the sweeteners, salt and preservatives in instant packets. Large bags of uncooked rice are another economical choice. Invest in an electric cooker for no-fuss preparation: simply rinse the rice, place it in the cooker, add water, and press the button. By the time you prepare the rest of the meal, your rice will be ready to eat!

12 Put on your baker's cap

The next time you need a birthday cake, breakfast scones, or batch of cookies for the PTA, resist the urge to run to the store. Make your own instead! For maximum savings, bake from scratch; flour, sugar, milk and butter are much less expensive than packaged mixes and ready-to-bake confections. Consider making your own bread as well; the aroma of a fresh-from-the-oven loaf is worth the effort alone! Because they have no preservatives or artificial ingredients, home-baked goods are healthier and tastier than store-bought ones. And they make wonderful, well-received—and inexpensive—gifts!

13 Design your own trail mix

Trail mix is a great, on-the-go snack, but buying it prepackaged can be expensive. Fortunately, it's cheap and easy to make your own, and your DIY mix won't have the added salt and sugar of commercial varieties. Best of all, you can fill it with your favorites, and leave out what you don't like. Ideas for ingredients include walnuts, cashews, almonds and pecans; dried cranberries, apricots, cherries and ginger; granola, raisins and sunflower seeds; and dark chocolate chips (in moderation!). Package in small containers or ziplock bags, and enjoy!

14 Design your own cereal

Commercial breakfast cereals come with high prices—and preservatives, sugar and sodium in every spoonful! Don't pay for the sprayed-on vitamins, fancy packaging and pricey advertising campaigns of name brand varieties. Make your own, healthier version for a fraction of the cost. Buy large boxes, or bulk quantities, of plain granola, flakes, or puffed rice; add your favorite nuts, seeds, and dried fruits to taste. Store in sealed containers for maximum freshness, and enjoy a delicious breakfast every morning—frugillionaire style!

15 Cut out the candy

Candy and sugary snacks put a dent in your wallet, and a bulge in your waistline! Don't waste hard-earned dollars on a box of empty calories. To get the most value from your food budget, focus on items that provide nutrition, sustenance, and the fuel your body needs—not a mouthful of sugar, chemicals and preservatives. Money spent on mass-market candy buys little more than colorful packaging and clever advertising; your body derives no benefit—and much potential harm—from its consumption. Satisfy your sweet tooth with a piece of fruit instead!

16 Dilute!

Fruit juice is expensive—and full of calories and sugar! Stretch it further by diluting it with water. Start out with 75% juice and 25% water, and adjust gradually to a 50/50 mix. You'll cut your juice expenditures in half, and may even prefer the taste. This frugillionaire technique has particular benefits for children. By diluting their juice, you'll reduce their cravings for sweet drinks, and decrease their sugar and calorie intake—thereby leaving room for more nutritious foods. For even greater savings, skip the juice entirely and buy whole fruits instead. They're less costly, and have more fiber and nutrients!

17 Make a menu

It takes a little time and effort, but planning meals is a proven money saver! Before your next shopping trip, sit down with pen and paper and make a menu for the week: include breakfast, lunch, dinner, snacks and beverages. If it helps, keep a database of meals on your computer, or write them on individual index cards. Take a quick inventory of your pantry and refrigerator, and make a list of needed ingredients. Planning ahead prevents overbuying, reduces waste, and inspires efficient use of food—like stretching a single chicken over several different meals. And when you know what you'll make for dinner, you're less likely to stop for takeout!

18 Shop with a list

Do you ever run into the grocery store for two or three things, and walk out with twenty? Somewhere between the milk and bananas, you discover a cartful of things you didn't realize you "needed!" Supermarkets are designed to promote impulse buying. High-margin, brightly packaged items are cleverly displayed to catch your eye and empty your wallet. Avoid the temptation by making a shopping list at home, and sticking to it when you get to the store. Instead of browsing, shop with laser-sharp focus: make a beeline for what's on the list, and you'll leave the store with your budget intact!

19 Shop less often

Avoid impulse buying at the grocery store by shopping less often. Try as we might to resist them, a few convenience foods—and other unnecessary items—manage to sneak their way into our carts each time we're there. The fewer visits we make, the less we're subject to temptation; and the more money we're able to keep in our wallets! Reduce shopping trips by planning meals ahead of time, and making a detailed list of what's needed. Eliminating last-minute runs to the supermarket saves on gas as well as food—a double blessing to your bank account!

20 Shop solo

If possible, go solo to the supermarket! The more family members that tag along, the more stuff that ends up in your cart. Children are particularly susceptible to clever marketing techniques. They're easily captivated by the bright colors and cartoon characters on candy, cereal and other impulse items, and will use all manner of persuasion to get you to purchase them. Adolescents and teens will likely add budget-busting convenience foods to your basket. Even spouses will slip in some extras, and it's much harder to say "no" to them! Shopping alone is faster, more efficient, and saves lots of money at the checkout!

21 Don't shop hungry

When our stomachs are growling, everything on the shelves is more enticing—even food we normally wouldn't buy! Marketers are well aware of this, and use clever techniques to stimulate our appetites: pleasing aromas at the store entrance, demonstration tables with tasty tidbits, and mouth-watering displays of bread, meats, cheeses and other fresh fare. Shore up your defenses by grocery shopping *after* a meal. At the very least, have a quick snack before heading to the store. When your stomach is full, your head is free to make more logical purchasing decisions!

22 Buy generic

Don't pay extra for a brand name or pretty package; the food inside is all that counts! The logo on the container may be the only difference between two cans of beans, cartons of juice, or boxes of cereal. Since many manufacturers make store brands as well as name brands, the product is often identical; yet the generic versions can be up to 50 percent cheaper! Read the labels and compare ingredients; you'll be surprised at the similarities. Famous brands get eye-level space, so look on lower or higher shelves for these bargains. You'll even find generics of organic and gourmet items!

23 Use coupons wisely

Coupons can save you a good chunk of change, as long as you use them wisely. Beware of those that are ads in disguise, tempting you to buy premium brands and processed convenience foods. Just because they're a dollar off, doesn't mean they're a good value! Even with a coupon, name brands may still cost more than store brands; do the math to make sure you're getting a good deal. To come out ahead, use coupons only for items you would have bought anyway. Save clipping time by going directly to manufacturers' websites, and printing out coupons for the products you use.

24 Shop by unit price

Shop by unit price—the cost per ounce, pound, liter, or other unit of measure—and you'll get more food for your money! Many stores provide this information alongside the price, helping you make easy comparisons between different sizes. If yours doesn't, whip out your calculator and divide the item's price by the amount in the container. For example, if a five-pound bag of sugar costs $3.00, the unit price is $0.60 per pound. If the ten-pound bag costs $5.00, it's only $0.50 per pound—a better bargain! But bigger doesn't always mean cheaper, so be sure to check the unit price before hauling home that super-sized jar of spaghetti sauce!

25 Buy in bulk—if it won't go to waste!

Suppose you've checked the unit price for a certain item, and determined that buying in bulk will save you money. Next ask yourself this question: will I be able to eat, drink, use or otherwise consume this item before it spoils or goes to waste? It's not a bargain if you wind up throwing half of it away! Unless you have a big family—or a very hearty appetite—play it safe and stick to non-perishables when buying in bulk. Stock up on toilet paper, canned goods, rice, pasta and beans if the price is right; but refrain from buying warehouse quantities of bread, meat, eggs, cheese or produce.

26 Brown bag your lunch

Consider this: if you go out to lunch five times per week, at a cost of $5-$10 a day, you'll spend a whopping $1300-$2600 over the course of the year! Instead, do as frugillionaires do: bring your own lunch to work, and put that extra thousand (or two!) into your bank account. Make a sandwich or salad at home for a fraction of what you'll pay at a restaurant or deli. Or cook a larger portion for dinner, refrigerate the leftovers, and enjoy a delicious feast of pasta, chicken, or vegetables the next afternoon. When you give up the fast food and lunches out, both your wallet and waistline benefit!

27 Bring your own snacks

Don't let workday munchies gobble up your paycheck; bring your own snacks, and avoid the vending machine! Those little bags of pretzels, cookies and chips command a hefty premium—often twice the grocery store price. You can slash this expense by planning ahead: buy economy sizes of your favorite treats, and pack a day's portion in a ziplock bag. Better yet, skip the junk food and opt for more nutritious fare like yogurt, raw veggies, crackers and cheese, or dried fruit and nuts. It's a healthier way to fend off hunger, while keeping your wallet nice and full!

28 Bring your own beverages

Instead of buying beverages from vending machines and convenience stores, bring them from home! It's much more economical to buy soda, juice and water in bulk than by the bottle. Purchasing by the gallon or case can yield significant discounts in terms of unit price. Use coupons, or shop at warehouse clubs, for even greater savings. It's also a good idea to carry a reusable bottle, and refill it from larger containers at home. That way, you can buy beverages in the most economical sizes, while enjoying the convenience of portable servings.

29 Enjoy alcohol in moderation

Limit your alcohol intake, for the sake of your finances and your health. If you're a frequent drinker, cut your cocktails to once a week, or have one glass of wine instead of two. It's easier to reduce your consumption than quit cold turkey; and when you do indulge, you'll enjoy it much more! It also pays to be adventurous when shopping for wine: explore lesser-known labels from around the world, and you'll find excellent bottles under $10. And when you're out on the town, remember that bar tabs and tips add up quickly. If you alternate cocktails with soda or water, you'll save money— and maybe your reputation!

30 Quench your thirst with water

Drinking water is one of the best things you can do for your body, and your bank account! Water is the ideal beverage for keeping your thirst quenched and your insides hydrated, and we're extremely fortunate to have a clean, on-demand supply of it coming from our faucets. Take advantage of this wonderful resource—it's significantly cheaper, healthier, and kinder to the environment than processed and packaged beverages. The recommended eight glasses of tap water a day costs around $1 per year—about the same price as a single soft drink!

31 Refill water bottles

When we're on the go, we often rely on bottled water to keep us refreshed. The problem: it's expensive to buy, and much of the plastic ends up in landfills. Fill reusable bottles with tap water instead; it's more eco-friendly, and can save you hundreds of dollars per year. Tap water in developed countries is typically clean and safe to drink; if contaminants are a concern, use a filtered pitcher or faucet attachment. Not ready to give up bottled water entirely? At least avoid the single servings. Buy the largest containers possible, and refill your reusable bottle.

32 Halve your restaurant habit

There's no doubt about it: dining out is expensive. The less we do it, the more we save—but we don't want to deny ourselves all the pleasures in life! Compromise, and cut your restaurant visits or takeout nights in half. If you usually eat out twice a week, reduce it to once; if you currently indulge just once a week, make it every other. Just like that, you'll have a fuller wallet—without feeling completely deprived. In fact, instead of being routine, going out for a restaurant meal will feel like a special occasion. You'll look forward to it with enthusiasm, and savor the experience!

33 Skip the appetizers—or make them a meal

Appetizers make big money for restaurants; smaller servings mean higher profits for them, and less value for you. To trim down your check, forgo them entirely. Most entrées are large enough to satisfy your hunger without the added expense, and calories, of a starter. Or, if the restaurant dishes out generous portions, order an appetizer as your main meal. Salads in particular can serve as light, healthy entrées. Furthermore, don't order multiple courses just to extend the length of your dining experience; eat a little more slowly instead!

34 Share an entrée

The next time you eat out, share an entrée with your dinner partner. Restaurant portions have grown substantially over the years, and can be several times larger than recommended serving sizes. Even if you split a meal, you're unlikely to leave the table hungry! While it's human nature to finish the food on your plate, you'd probably feel just as satisfied with a smaller amount. If you really want to indulge, share an appetizer and dessert with your partner as well. You'll enjoy a wonderful feast—with half the calories, and half the bill!

35 Skip (or share) dessert

You know the saying: a moment on the lips, forever on the hips. A restaurant dessert serves up a double whammy: it plumps up the bill as well as your body. Low-cost ingredients like sugar, flour and butter mean high profit margins for restaurants. That's why the waiter swoops in with that tempting tray of sweets after your meal! If you have the fortitude, wait until you get home and have a piece of antioxidant-rich dark chocolate. Alternatively, order *one* dessert for the table; most are large enough, and rich enough, to serve several people. A few bites will usually satisfy your sweet tooth!

36 BYOB

For big savings, frequent restaurants that let you bring your own bottle of wine. Alcohol is a major profit maker for dining establishments, and the markup on wine lists is staggering: typically 200 to 300 percent per bottle. Buying wine by the glass is even more expensive. Fortunately, the BYOB concept is popular among aspiring restaurateurs, as it allows them to break into the business without the expense of a liquor license. When you patronize these smaller, independent eateries, you'll not only save money on alcohol; you'll enjoy a more unique culinary experience!

37 Try the house wine

Even if your dinner spot is not BYOB, you can still save money on alcohol by ordering the house wine. In the past, house wines were often chosen by price rather than quality, and therefore not highly regarded. But these days, they're considered part of a restaurant's image; and most places won't risk their reputations by serving a poor one. Sommeliers take pride in their selections, seeking wines that are high in quality, reasonably priced, and complementary to the cuisine. Ask for a taste before committing to a carafe — then drink a toast to your savings!

38 Use restaurant coupons

Stretch your dining-out dollars with restaurant coupons! Eateries offer them to attract new customers and drum up business during slow periods; look for them in local newspapers and ad mailers. You can also find great dining deals on the internet. Restaurant.com, for example, sells certificates for participating establishments at deep discounts. At the time of this writing, you can purchase a $25 voucher for only $10 (some restrictions apply). Just pay for it, print it, and take it to the restaurant. First dates aside, it's a great way to avoid leaving money on the table!

39 Have a fancy lunch

Dying to try that new four-star restaurant? Avoid the sticker shock by going for lunch! The portions are smaller, and the fare lighter, meaning minimal waste and leftovers. Better yet, the atmosphere is usually less stuffy, making for a more relaxing experience. In fact, it feels fabulous, and a little decadent, to indulge in a fancy lunch; no one will suspect frugality as your motivation! Use this strategy the next time you're considering a splurge at some culinary hot spot. When you dine like a frugillionaire, you can eat well without breaking the bank!

40 Revive the lost art of picnicking

Picnics are a fabulous way to eat "out"—without the restaurant expense! They evolved from medieval outdoor banquets, and were a favorite pastime of European royalty. Embrace this grand tradition, and organize an outing of your own. Your picnic fare can be as simple as bread, cheese, olives and finger food. Sandwiches and salads are also easy to pack, transport and eat with a minimum of fuss. Alternatively, fix an entire feast to enjoy al fresco; just be sure to keep foods appropriately hot or cold to prevent spoilage. If you don't want to cook, many grocery stores offer prepared meals that are picnic-perfect!

41 Have a potluck dinner party

Forgo the restaurant, and invite friends over for a potluck dinner party! Ask everyone to bring a dish, and serve the contributions buffet style. Assign each person a category in advance—appetizer, entrée, side dish, or dessert—to ensure an appropriate variety. A theme provides consistency and increases the fun: some ideas include comfort food, childhood favorites, and ethnic cuisine (like Indian, Chinese or Italian). A potluck is not only less expensive than going out for a meal; it gives everyone a chance to show off their culinary skills, and share their favorite recipes!

42 Have cocktails at home

Bar tabs add up quickly when you're out with friends for cocktails! Grab some six-packs of beer, or bottles of wine, and party at home instead. Don't worry about full-scale catering; set out a simple spread of bread, cheese, crackers, chips, pretzels and other snacks. Connect your iPod to the stereo for cheap entertainment, and encourage guests with mp3 players to join in providing the music. It's a great way to socialize without the crowds, bar tab or tips! Just remember to be a responsible host, and make sure nobody drinks and drives.

43 Limit the lattes

A daily latte from the coffee shop is a big budget-buster; that $3 a day adds up to over $1000 a year! If it's the experience you savor, cut down your visits to once a week. Being a frugillionaire isn't about deprivation, but appreciation: when the visits are no longer routine, you'll savor them as a special treat. If the coffee is what you crave, invest in a high-quality machine and make your own—it'll pay for itself in no time. Or share the cost of one for the office with latte-loving coworkers, and take turns buying the beans!

44 Dine with cloth napkins

Limit your use of disposable products, such as paper napkins; it's like throwing your cash in the trash! Dine with cloth napkins instead; they're cheaper in the long run, and make your table look like a million bucks! You can purchase them inexpensively from discount and dollar stores. Better yet, make your own, using remnants from the fabric store or material you have around the house. Simply measure the pieces, cut into squares, and hem the edges. They lend an elegant touch to your dining room, and help you save money with style!

45 Fire up the grill, and keep your cool

Everyone loves a barbecue, and using the grill can slash your utility bills! By cooking out on warm summer nights, you'll avoid turning on the oven, heating up the house, and running the air conditioner to cool it down. And you'll have a blast preparing, and eating, your dinner al fresco! You can also keep your cool by using toaster ovens, crock pots and microwaves in warm weather; they heat only the meal, and not the whole house. Alternatively, serve up cold foods on hot days: sandwiches, salads and fruits are lighter, more refreshing summer fare that won't raise the temperature in your kitchen.

46 Track your food spending

It's easy to forget about those deli lunches and takeout dinners—then wonder where your money's gone! But there's a sure-fire way to stay on budget: write down what you spend. Use a notebook or computer spreadsheet to record food-related purchases, be they from supermarkets, restaurants, convenience stores or vending machines. List *everything*, no matter how small; include those bottles of water, bags of chips, and your daily pastrami sandwich. At the end of each week, review your expenditures. When it's all in front of you, you'll see exactly where you can trim the fat!

Chapter 2

HOME EXPENSES

Slashing Utility Costs and Shrinking Your Bills

---

47 Small is beautiful

Frugillionaires know that a bigger home isn't necessarily better: who wants to spend all their time dusting, mopping and vacuuming thousands of square feet? We have more fabulous things to do! Trade down to a smaller house or apartment. You'll have less clutter, less to maintain, less to clean—and much more free time. In fact, you'll be surprised how much money you save when you have a smaller space. You'll not only decrease your utility bills, you'll lower your overall spending—because you can't purchase things when you have no place to put them!

48 Do it yourself

The next time something breaks around the house, save some money and fix it yourself! Attend workshops at hardware stores to learn basic skills and become familiar with the tools of the trade. For project-specific instructions, consult books on home repair or search the internet. Start with easier tasks—like fixing a leaky faucet or unclogging a toilet—and tackle bigger jobs as you gain experience. If you have the time and inclination, try a home improvement project like painting, wallpapering, installing moldings, or replacing plumbing or lighting fixtures. You'll add value to your house, without the cost of a contractor.

49 Do preventative maintenance

Maintain your house and appliances to avoid costly repairs in the future. Following are a few ways to help keep your home in tip-top shape. Inspect your HVAC filter monthly, and replace if necessary; clean your clothes dryer vent regularly; and vacuum the coils of your refrigerator twice a year. Remove debris from gutters and downspouts, and make sure they're working properly to keep water away from your foundation. Inspect your roof, and replace damaged shingles before leaks occur. Hire professionals to check your furnace and fireplace on a yearly basis. And don't forget to change the batteries in your smoke and carbon monoxide detectors!

50 See the light

Replace traditional incandescent light bulbs with compact fluorescents—and save big bucks on your electric bill! Compact fluorescent light bulbs (CFLs) use about 75 percent less energy than incandescent ones, and last about ten times longer. They also produce less heat, helping you save on home cooling costs. CFLs are available in a variety of sizes and shapes to fit almost any light fixture. They cost more than traditional bulbs, but pay for themselves quickly in reduced energy bills. They're particularly convenient for hard-to-reach fixtures, since they seldom need replacing!

51 Turn down the thermostat in winter

Consider this: for every degree you lower your thermostat, you can save from 1 to 3 percent on your heating bill. Set your thermostat at 68 degrees Fahrenheit when you're at home and awake, and lower it while at work or asleep; turning it down 10 degrees for eight hours can slash your heating costs by 10 percent. While you're saving money, stay warm like a frugillionaire: put on your coziest sweater, enjoy a hot cup of tea, bundle under extra blankets, or snuggle up with your sweetheart. And when the snow is falling, or wind howling, be ever so grateful for the roof over your head!

52 Turn up the thermostat in summer

If you have central air conditioning, use a similar strategy in summer: set your thermostat at 78 degrees Fahrenheit when you're at home, and turn it up while you're away. Don't keep your house so cold that you need to wear a sweater in July! Save further on cooling costs by installing ceiling and window fans to circulate air throughout the house, and an attic fan to exhaust warm air to the outdoors. In spring and fall, open the windows instead of turning on the A/C. And in the dog days of summer, beat the heat in true Southern style: sip an iced tea or mint julep, and catch some cool breezes on the porch!

53 Get a programmable thermostat

Buy a programmable thermostat; it'll save you a bundle on utility bills, and pay for itself in no time. You can set different temperatures for different times of the day—like when you're at home, at work, or asleep. That way, you won't have to remember to adjust it yourself. Best of all, you can have it turn up the heat an hour before you wake—making it much easier to get out of bed on cold winter mornings. Most have separate weekend modes, so you'll rarely need to make a manual adjustment. With a programmable thermostat, you can maximize your comfort, and your savings, with nary a second thought!

54 Dodge drafts

Plug the air leaks in your home, and you'll lower your utility bills. The areas around doors and windows are notorious for letting cold air enter in winter, and air conditioning escape in summer. Test for drafts by holding a lit candle near suspect locations; if the flame flickers, you've found a leak! Use caulk or weather stripping to fill any cracks or holes, and seal around window and door frames. Stop airflow under doors with draft dodgers and sweeps, and insulate windows with heavy curtains, blankets or plastic film. Electrical outlets can also leak cold air into your home; seal them with foam gaskets, which are inexpensive and easy to install.

55 Add insulation

Add insulation—it's one of the most effective ways to reduce energy costs. Insulation stops heat loss in winter, and heat gain in summer, helping to maintain a comfortable temperature inside your home. Start in your attic, where installation is easiest and usually results in the greatest savings. An R-38 insulation value (about 12-15 inches thick) is commonly recommended; colder climates require more. Reduce heating and cooling costs further by insulating your basement or crawlspace, and inside your walls. An added bonus: some states and utilities offer tax credits and rebates for properly insulated homes.

56 Lower your water heater's temperature

Your water heater uses energy to maintain a constant temperature: the lower that temperature, the lower your energy costs. According to the U. S. Department of Energy, you can save 3 to 5 percent for every 10 degree decrease in water temperature. Check the thermostat: they're often set to 140 degrees Fahrenheit by default, while 120 degrees Fahrenheit is sufficient for most household use (some dishwashers require higher heat, so consult your manual first). A lower temperature also reduces the danger of scalding, and slows corrosion in your pipes. When you're away from home for an extended period, turn the water heater to its lowest setting, or turn it off completely.

57 Insulate your hot water heater

If your water heater tank is warm to the touch, wrap it with a special insulating blanket; they're pre-cut, inexpensive and available at most hardware stores. Some utility companies even sell and install them at low cost. Insulating electric water heaters is pretty straightforward; just follow the instructions carefully, and be sure not to cover the thermostat. Gas and oil-fired water heaters present a greater challenge, because of the flue and pilot light; professional installation is usually recommended. The Department of Energy estimates that insulation can save 4 to 9 percent in water heating costs—while providing you with nice, hot showers!

58 Use energy- and water-saving appliances

When it's time to replace old appliances, select energy- and water-efficient models for big savings. ENERGY STAR—a joint program of the U. S. Department of Energy and the Environmental Protection Agency—helps you make smart choices by identifying products of superior efficiency. Look for the "ENERGY STAR" label when purchasing refrigerators, clothes washers, air conditioners, dishwashers, boilers, furnaces, lighting, computer equipment, home electronics and more. These appliances use 10 to 50 percent less energy and water than conventional models, and can dramatically lower your utility bills!

59 Do full loads

Always do full loads of laundry—you'll save water, power, money and time! Partial loads use the same amount of energy as full loads, and can also waste water. This doesn't mean you should overload the washer; just schedule your laundry so you'll run as few cycles as possible. Such planning also reduces wear and tear on your machine, increasing its lifespan and decreasing the need for costly repairs. Do the same with your dishwasher: stick to full loads for the most efficient use of energy, water and detergent. If your dirty dishes are few, wash them by hand and save the electricity.

60 Wash towels less often

Here's an idea that will save you money *and* time: wash bath towels less often. They really don't need laundering on a daily basis; you're clean when you use them, after all! Give yourself and your utilities a break, and let them go three to four days—or even a week—between washings. But take note: this strategy won't work if the towels are piled on the bathroom floor. Hang them immediately after use (and instruct family members to do the same!), so they dry thoroughly and stay fresh. This simple habit will lessen your laundry, lower your bills, and lighten your workload!

61 Dry wisely

Air-drying laundry is best—but not always practical due to the weather, or time constraints. When you use your dryer, try the following tips to save energy and money. Do full loads rather than partial ones, since they use similar amounts of energy. Run multiple loads one after another to take advantage of residual heat. Use the moisture sensor instead of the timer; it monitors the humidity in the drum, and turns off the machine automatically when clothes are dry. Clean the lint filter after every load, to improve efficiency and reduce the risk of fire. And when the sun comes out—hang up your clothesline!

62 Air-dry dishes

Let your dishes air-dry—it's one of the simplest ways to slash energy bills. If your dishwasher has one, use the "air-dry" setting; if not, skip the "heat-dry" cycle and turn it off after the final rinse. Open the door and pull out the racks, to let air circulate through the contents. It couldn't be any easier! Just be sure that dishes are completely dry before putting them away, as stacking them wet encourages bacteria growth. Air-drying takes a little more time, but no extra effort. You'll save electricity, money, and the environment— without lifting a finger!

63 Pull the plug on energy leaks

When you turn off home electronics, you expect the power to stop flowing—but that's not always the case! Televisions, stereos, DVD players, computers, kitchen appliances and cell phone chargers continually drain electricity, just by being plugged into the wall. These little leaks (or "phantom loads") can add up to big bucks on your electric bill. For frugillionaires, it's second nature to turn off the lights when leaving a room. Do the same with unused devices! Make it easy to "pull the plug" by grouping multiple items onto power strips; that way, you can save money with a simple flick of a switch.

64 Control exterior lights

Don't leave exterior lights burning all day and night. Put them on timers instead, and program lights to turn on and off at predetermined hours. Some fixtures include (or can be fitted with) photo sensors, which automatically switch lights on at dusk, and shut them off at sunrise. For even greater savings, install outdoor lights with motion sensors. They activate only when movement is detected—providing safety and security, without illuminating the entire perimeter of your home. Finally, exercise restraint with ornamental lighting—or turn it on only when you're outside to enjoy it!

65 Don't let the water run

Don't pour money down the drain—turn off the water while brushing your teeth! It's a simple change in routine, but the cumulative effect—twice a day, every day—can mean big savings on your water bill. Get the whole family on board for maximum impact; it's a wonderful habit for children to learn. Save while you shave with a similar technique: use a little water for wetting, turn it off while lathering, then on again only to rinse. Miss the background noise while performing your daily ablutions? Turn on some music instead of the faucet—it's more fun, frugal, and environmentally-friendly.

66 Go with the low-flow

Install a low-flow showerhead; it's good for the planet, and your wallet. While traditional showerheads use 5 to 8 gallons per minute, low-flow versions use 2.5 or less—saving several gallons of water each minute of your shower. But wait—there's more! Warm showers require gas or electricity to heat the water; when you reduce the amount of water, you also reduce your energy use. The result: two bills slashed with one simple device! Low-flow fixtures are readily available at hardware and home improvement stores, and easy to install. With the latest technology, you won't even feel a difference in water pressure.

67 Shorten your shower

According to the Environmental Protection Agency, 17 percent of our indoor water use is devoted to showering. Imagine all those drops as pennies, going down the drain—and save that money by taking shorter showers! Cut them down to five minutes by focusing on the task at hand: wash, shampoo and rinse. Save extra rituals like shaving, brushing your teeth, or singing an aria for when the water isn't running. If you lose track of time while lathering up, set a kitchen timer; or play a single song on a CD player, and try to finish before it's over. Since showers account for roughly two-thirds of water heating costs, you'll also lower your energy bill.

68 Make faucets frugal

Save gallons of water each day by equipping faucets with low-flow aerators. Install them in your kitchen and bathrooms, and you'll waste much less water washing hands and dishes. About 2 to 5 gallons of water flow through standard faucets each minute; low-flow aerators dramatically reduce this rate. For maximum efficiency, choose aerators of 1 gallon per minute or less. Pick them up inexpensively at your local hardware store—installation is a snap, and they pay for themselves in no time. You'll not only save money on water, but also the energy used to heat it!

69 Check for stealth leaks

Leaks don't always have a telltale "drip." They can stay behind the scenes, stealthily wasting your water—and your money! Fortunately, you can catch these culprits with a simple test. Turn off all faucets and water-using appliances like sinks, showers, dishwashers, clothes washers and sprinklers. Check your water meter: if the hand is moving, there's a leak in the system. If it's still, note the position. Refrain from water use for 30 minutes, then return for a second reading. If it's the same, you're in the clear; but if it's moved, you've discovered a leak. To pinpoint the problem, check faucets, toilets and appliances; or pick up the phone and call a plumber!

70 Fix leaky faucets

Don't let a leaky faucet drain your wallet! The most common cause is a worn-out washer, o-ring or cartridge that simply needs to be replaced. It's a repair most frugillionaires can do themselves, without paying a professional plumber. Simply shut off the water supply to the sink, plug the drain, and disassemble the faucet handle; as you remove parts, make note of their order, so you can put it back together. See plumbing repair books and websites for detailed instructions. If you're unsure what needs replacing, take the entire assembly to your local hardware store. They'll help you diagnose the problem and find the right parts.

71 Test for toilet leaks

If you have high water bills, suspect a leaky toilet. Don't assume all is well just because the floor is dry; the problem isn't always obvious. There's a simple test you can do to make sure your money isn't going…well, you know where! Remove the cover from the tank, and add a dye tablet or food coloring to the water inside. Then let the toilet sit, unused, for half an hour. If any dyed water makes its way into the bowl, you have a leaky loo! For tips on how to find—and fix—the failing part, consult the internet, a home repair book, or your favorite plumber.

72 Get a low-flow loo

Replace your older toilet with a low-flow model, and you'll see the difference in your water bill! Most toilets made before 1994 use 3.5 to 7 gallons of water per flush; low-flow commodes, on the other hand, use just 1.6 gallons or less. The savings add up each trip to the loo! Poor-performing early models gave these "green" latrines a bad rap; but they've come a long way since first introduced. Improvements in design and technology, such as dual-flush and pressure-assisted systems, ensure a successful and satisfying flush. Do your research before making a purchase: you can find toilet performance ratings and reviews on the internet, and in consumer magazines.

73 Make baths a luxury

The Environmental Protection Agency estimates that we use about 70 gallons of water for a full bath, versus 10-25 gallons for a five-minute shower. That's all well and good—but sometimes we just need a nice soak. Indulge occasionally—rather than regularly—and you'll appreciate it all the more. To minimize water waste, plug the drain as soon as you turn on the faucet. The initial cold water will be brought up to temperature as the flow becomes warmer. Fill the bath half-full, or just enough to immerse your body; add bubbles to give the illusion of a fuller tub. When you make baths a luxurious treat, you can still save money—by skipping the spa!

74 Cut the cable

Drop the expensive cable, fiber optic or satellite television services—and put your money, and time, to better use! You won't miss much: news is readily available on the internet, and DVDs can be rented (or borrowed from the library) when you're in the mood for a movie. If you're not ready to go cold turkey, cut back to basic service without the premium channels. You'll waste a lot less time flicking through stations, only to discover there's nothing good on. Use the time after dinner to read a book, hang out with your family, or take a walk instead. "Real life" is infinitely more interesting!

75 Bundle up

Save money by purchasing telephone, television and high-speed internet services from the same company. Such "bundled" deals typically cost much less than purchasing them individually. Just be aware that some packages are limited-time offers—so keep an eye on your bill at the end of the period. If it rises substantially, shop around for another provider; chances are, you'll be able to get a competitive rate through a different company. But give your original provider a call before you make your move. They may offer you another year at the same price, simply to keep you from switching.

76 Slow down your internet service

If you do little more on the internet than check your email and surf the web, don't pay extra for lightning-speed service. Many broadband providers offer tiered pricing for different speeds; try a slower one, and see if you notice the difference. You may not mind waiting a fraction of a second longer for your messages to download, and you can save up to $20 a month. If you're not online often—and you're blessed with the virtue of patience—consider downgrading to dial-up service. It's slow, but it's cheap; and if you don't mind seeing some ads on your screen, you can even get it for free!

77 Cut the phone frills

Take a close look at your phone bill: are you paying for features you don't use or don't need? Many packages are bundled with caller id, call waiting, call forwarding, three-way calling, voice mail and more. You're billed for them, whether you use them or not! Call your provider, and ask the price of a basic, no-frills telephone line. If one (or more) of the extras is important to you, see if it's cheaper to buy a la carte. And if you mainly use your cell phone, strip your landline to the bone; you're unlikely to need the premium services.

78 Make calls over the internet

If you have a reliable broadband connection, consider using VoIP (Voice over IP) for telephone service. This technology converts your voice to digital signals and sends them over the internet; to use it, you'll need a computer, adaptor or specialized phone. VoIP packages—offered by companies like Skype and Vonage—are typically much cheaper than conventional phone plans, particularly for long-distance calls. In fact, you can often talk to people on the same network free of charge! The drawbacks: VoIP phones may not connect directly to 9-1-1 emergency centers, and won't work during internet and power outages. Take these issues into account before replacing your traditional phone service.

79 Use free 411

Dialing 411 for directory assistance is expensive—usually around $1-$2 per call! Save money by looking up numbers in the phone book, or on the internet, instead. If you're on the road, use free directory assistance services like 1-800-FREE-411 or 1-800-411-METRO. The catch: you'll have to listen to a few ads before receiving your information. Google, the internet search engine, offers free 411 business listings at 1-800-GOOG-411. The number you request is sent by text message, and the call is automatically connected.

80 Use prepaid phone cards

If you make long distance calls only on occasion, consider using prepaid phone cards—it may be more economical than paying for a monthly service. Cards are typically available in $5, $10, $20 or $50 increments, and are valid for a certain amount of talk time (measured in minutes). They're easy to use: simply call the toll-free access number, enter the PIN number printed on the card, then dial the phone number to which you want to connect. Per-minute rates are usually very competitive; just be sure to select a card with no connection or maintenance fees. Prepaid cards are particularly useful for "budgeting" long distance costs, and avoiding surprises on your phone bill!

81 Lose the landline

Do you have enough cell phone minutes to cover all your local and long-distance calls? If the answer is yes, drop your landline! With taxes and fees, a basic line can cost $20-$30 each month (not including long distance); that's hundreds of dollars per year in potential savings! Other advantages to the cell-only life include less risk of missing important phone calls; freedom from telemarketers; and the ability to keep your phone number wherever you move. The one drawback is the inability of 9-1-1 responders to pinpoint your location when you call; the Federal Communications Commission is currently addressing this issue.

82 Review your cell phone plan

Review your cell phone bills, to make sure your plan gives you the best bang for your buck. Consider downgrading if you have lots of leftover minutes each month. Or, if you often exceed your allotment, think about upgrading—it may be more economical than paying costly overage fees. Look into family plans if more than one member of your household carries a phone; additional lines can be added for as little as $10 per month. You can also save minutes, and money, with in-network calling: sign up with the same provider as your friends and family, and you may be able to talk to them at little to no cost!

83 Get a prepaid cell phone

If you use your cell phone infrequently—or keep it only for emergencies—consider a prepaid plan. Regular plans typically cost between $30-$60 per month; if you don't use all the minutes, you leave money on the table. With prepaid plans, you pay only for the minutes you use, and simply purchase more when you run low. Per-minute rates are typically higher, so they're not for those with the gift of gab. But if you don't make many calls, such plans can yield significant savings. Other benefits: they don't require a credit check, and you won't need to worry about long-term service contracts.

84 Drop the data plan

Data and entertainment plans can add $10-$50 per month to your cell phone bill; question if you really need them. Must you be able to send email and browse the web when away from your home or office? Is it worth the extra money to watch videos, play games, or listen to music on your phone? If some features are necessary for work, see if your employer will pick up the tab. Otherwise, calculate how much you'll save without them—and then decide how important they are. If you're unsure, drop these extra services temporarily to see if you miss them. You may even find some serenity in being less "connected!"

85 Shop around for homeowner's insurance

Whether you're looking for a new policy, or reviewing your current one, shop around for the best rate on homeowner's or renter's insurance. Ask friends and family for recommendations, or seek help from your state's insurance department. You can also get details on pricing and customer service—and find out an insurer's reputation for handling claims—from consumer guides and insurance agents. And don't forget the internet: online quote services make it easy to compare offerings from different companies. Shopping for insurance may not be the most enjoyable task, but it can free up hundreds of dollars for more pleasurable pursuits!

86 Raise your deductible

Reduce your insurance bill by raising your deductible; you may be able to save 10 to 30 percent off your current rates (ask your insurer for details). The deductible is the amount of money *you* must pay toward a loss, before your insurer covers the claim. For example, if your home incurs $1000 worth of damage—and you have a $250 deductible—your insurance pays only $750. The higher your deductible, the lower your premiums. Just make sure you have enough money in an emergency fund to cover the deductible amount; you won't save anything if you have to pay it with a credit card!

87 Be a loyal insurance customer

Most companies offer discounted rates if you consolidate your insurance policies with them. Buy your home and automobile coverage from the same insurer, and you can save 5 to 15 percent on premiums. Do the math, and verify that combining policies costs less than purchasing them from separate companies. Staying with the same insurer for a number of years can also pay off. Some companies reward long-term policyholders with lower premiums; others grant dividends to their customers if they've experienced strong financial performance, or a less-than-expected number of claims.

88 Review your riders

Standard homeowner's policies don't always provide full coverage for high-value possessions, such as jewelry, artwork, electronics and computers. You can purchase extra insurance for them—to cover theft, damage, or loss—in the form of a rider (also called an endorsement or floater). Review your riders periodically to make sure you're not paying unnecessary premiums. Some items, such as furs or computer equipment, may have depreciated with age. Others may have been sold, or given to friends and family. Henceforth, try this frugillionare strategy: don't buy as many valuables. You'll save on both the purchase price, and insurance costs!

89 Secure your home

Add safety and security features to your home. They not only protect your family and improve your peace of mind, they save you money on insurance! Many companies offer discounts if you equip your home with a burglar alarm, fire extinguisher, smoke detectors and deadbolt locks. You'll lower your premiums even more by installing a home security system with external monitoring—the kind that automatically calls the police or fire station when the alarm is triggered. Such systems can be expensive, though; be sure to ask your insurer what type meets their requirements and earns you the largest discounts.

90 Consider insurance when house hunting

If you're in the market for a new home, include insurance costs in your decision process. The materials from which a house is built affect the premium: you'll often get a price break for less flammable substances, like masonry walls and metal roofs. Find out how the age of the house—and its electrical, plumbing, and HVAC systems—will impact the insurance rate, and consider if you'll have to upgrade such systems to obtain adequate (and affordable) coverage. Geography is another important factor: insurance costs are significantly higher in areas prone to flooding, earthquakes or other natural disasters.

91 Review your private mortgage insurance

Lenders require private mortgage insurance (PMI) for home loans greater than 80 percent of a property's value. PMI protects the bank should you default on your loan—but it's an extra expense for you! When your home equity reaches 20 percent, request that the policy be cancelled immediately. Paying the premium for even one extra month is a waste of your money. Keep an eye on your loan amortization table, so you'll know when you've repaid 20 percent of the principal. If you've done major improvements, or your house has appreciated in value, consider having it re-appraised; you may have earned enough equity to drop the PMI.

92 Challenge your property tax assessment

You may be able to save big money by challenging your property tax assessment. For a successful appeal, you'll need to show that your house has been overvalued. You'll have a strong case if comparable houses in your neighborhood have lower assessments, or if the assessor has made errors in evaluating your property—like overstating the square footage, or number of bedrooms and baths. Research public property records, or enlist the help of a real estate agent, to gather supporting data. It's worth the effort to learn the appeals process in your community; it may be easier than you think to save hundreds (or even thousands) of dollars each year!

Chapter 3

HOME DÉCOR

Creating a Stylish Home
on a Shoestring

---

93 Sell your clutter

If you have stuff you never use, no longer want, or are just plain tired of looking at sell it! You'll gain space in your home, and cash in your wallet. If you have a large quantity of low-priced items, hold a yard sale. Increase the traffic, and fun, by inviting neighbors to join you. To unload more unique, collectible or valuable castoffs, turn to the internet: try online classifieds (such as Craigslist.com) or auctions (like eBay.com). You can even sell used books, CDs, DVDs and other goods through retail giant Amazon.com. Surf the web to find out what your stuff's worth, and then decide if you'd rather have the cash!

94 Get creative with your furniture

Your home doesn't need new designer furniture to look fabulous! In fact, a well-edited mix of vintage, hand-me-down and repurposed pieces is much more interesting than a sterile showroom look. Old trunks make wonderful storage and coffee tables. A dresser can be reused as a buffet or sideboard. Add a set of legs to turn an old door, or piece of countertop, into a stylish desk. Even milk crates can function as bookshelves, TV stands and end tables; cover them with fabric for a decorator look. To stretch your budget further, invest in pieces that do double-duty: like sleeper sofas, or tables and ottomans with built-in storage.

95 Embrace furniture with a past

Furnish your home frugally with pre-owned pieces! For terrific bargains, try thrift shops, consignment stores, and garage sales—or even the sidewalks on bulk trash day! You can also find cheap (and free) furnishings online; browse Craigslist.com and Freecycle.com for local offerings. And don't forget to alert friends and family to your needs; most people have a piece or two they'd be happy to pass along. To spruce up older items, add a fresh coat of paint or stylish hardware. Secondhand sofas and chairs can be re-upholstered, or slipcovered, for a brand-new look.

96 Sit on the floor

Instead of splurging on sofas, loveseats, recliners and chairs—sit on the floor! It's the norm for many cultures around the world. Simply toss around cushions for extra seating; you'll set a more relaxed, bohemian mood, and free up floor space for other activities. You may even be able to dine at your coffee table, and forgo investing in a table and chairs; just look to Japanese homes for inspiration. If you're worried about guest seating, keep a few folding chairs stored away for when you have visitors. You'll love the increased functionality, and uncluttered look, of your space!

97 Use what you already own

Pass on the pricey décor, and adorn your house with what you already own! To arrange your stuff artistically, use a favorite technique of interior designers: group like items together, instead of scattering them throughout a room. A row of glass bottles or stack of vintage books packs more visual punch than solitary items. Personal mementos make particularly charming displays: create vignettes with your grandmother's china, father's pipes, childhood items, travel souvenirs, or other sentimental keepsakes. It's more beautiful, meaningful—and frugal—than store-bought décor!

98 Mix high and low

A beautiful house need not be filled exclusively with expensive designer pieces. Even decorators and celebrities prefer to mix highbrow items with discount store treasures and flea market finds. It makes a home more interesting, and reflects the style and creativity of its owner. If you want, splurge on one item that will be the focal point of a room—such as a sofa, bed or special piece of art. Then use less expensive pieces to fill out the décor. If you stick to a certain theme, style or color palette, it'll all work together; and you won't feel like you live in a stuffy showroom!

99 Go cheap and chic

Look for chic pieces in unlikely places, and save a bundle adorning your home! Expensive boutiques aren't the only purveyors of stylish décor. Ikea is a wonderland of low-cost, well-designed furniture and accessories; and budget retailers like Target, Marshalls and TJ Maxx offer deep discounts on interior accents. Shop home improvement centers for light fixtures, decorative hardware, shelving and window treatments. You'll find items nearly identical to those in specialty stores and catalogs—at much lower prices. Check out craft supply outlets for bargains on baskets, vases, frames, candles and floral arrangements.

100 Steal some ideas

Get a design education on a dime, by browsing home décor magazines and catalogs. It's a wonderful, low-cost way to learn basic decorating techniques: like how to combine color and texture, lay out furniture, display collections and arrange shelves. So go ahead and be a copycat; just don't buy the expensive designer goods! Use the images as a guide, and work with what you have—or can acquire on the cheap—to create a similar look. Magazines regularly feature the work of the hottest interior decorators. Steal their ideas for your own home, and you'll benefit from their creative genius—without having to pay their consultation fees!

101 Change the backdrop

Your home is the stage on which your daily life plays out. Instead of adding more props, consider changing the backdrop! A coat of paint is the easiest, cheapest and most dramatic way to transform a room. To save time and money, apply color on one accent wall rather than all of them. If you prefer wallpaper, a border or mural can have the desired effect—at less cost than covering the entire room. Add architectural interest by installing crown moldings, or decorative trim around windows and doors. A simple background change can be the most effective—and frugal—way to spice up your space!

102 Explore frugal flooring options

Wondering how to replace that old shag carpet or linoleum tile—without spending a fortune? The solution depends on what lies beneath. Hardwood floors can be exposed without the expense of refinishing; simply cover rough spots with furniture or throw rugs. Plywood can be painted in solid colors, patterns or artistic effects. If you prefer carpet, purchase remnants instead of wall-to-wall; they're often large enough to cover an entire room, and can be cut to size with a utility knife. Or check out the new choices in laminate flooring and vinyl tiles: they give your floors the look of wood, ceramic or stone, without the expense!

103 Go natural

Let Mother Nature help decorate your house! Instead of buying mass-produced seasonal items, go outside for inspiration. Take a nature walk, and see what beautiful freebies you can collect. Adorn your home with acorns, pumpkins, and colorful leaves in fall; and evergreens, holly, and pinecones in winter. Display fresh and dried flowers in spring, and seashells and ornamental grasses in summer. For a fresh look in kitchen and dining areas, set out a bowl of brightly colored fruit (like apples, oranges or lemons). Or fill glass containers with rocks and pebbles to create modern, organic décor—on a frugillionaire budget!

104 Get crafty

Skip the store-bought décor, and make your own! With a little creativity, you can beautify your home on a shoestring budget. Fill a glass bowl with colored marbles, or floating votives, for a sophisticated centerpiece. Paint or decoupage tiles from the hardware store, and use them to give new life to a tired tabletop. Buy unfinished items from craft supply stores—like boxes, vases, baskets, or candleholders—and customize them to match your décor. If you're short on skills, or lack inspiration, browse through craft magazines and websites—they're treasure troves of ideas, instructions and tutorials.

105 Decorate with fabric

Even if you can't sew, you can still decorate with fabric! You'll find plenty of instructions on the internet for no-sew pillow covers, tablecloths, runners, placemats and more. Use iron-on tape, or fabric glue, to finish edges and apply decorative trim. Velcro, or grommets and ribbon, are no-fuss alternatives to buttonholes for closures. You can even reupholster dining chairs easily and cheaply; all you need is fabric and a staple gun. Just be careful not to blow your budget on expensive textiles: buy discounted remnants, or use bed sheets and fabric paint. Add tassels, cord and fringe for a luxurious, decorator look.

106 Make your own curtains

Buying window treatments for your home can cost a small fortune. But if you can live without frills, flounces and other frippery, it's easy (and inexpensive) to make your own curtains! First, find a piece of fabric you like, and cut it to the appropriate size. Then create a hem at the bottom, and a rod pocket at the top, by sewing a simple straight stitch or using iron-on tape. Alternatively: fold a pretty sheet, tablecloth, or scarf over a curtain rod, or hang it up with drapery clips. If you don't want to spring for hardware, attach the fabric directly to the wall with upholstery tacks.

107 Make your own headboard

Create a look of luxury in your boudoir—by making a gorgeous upholstered headboard! Select a fabric to fit the mood: like casual cotton, romantic silk, funky vinyl or fake fur. You'll also need a ¼" piece of plywood, 2" thick foam, and batting or fiberfill. Make a sandwich with the fabric right side down, then the batting, foam and board on top. Wrap the fabric and batting around the plywood, and secure to the back with a staple gun. Use flush mounts (heavy duty picture hangers) to attach the finished headboard to the wall. Search the internet for complete instructions and design inspiration.

108 Make your own duvet cover

Freshen up your bedroom décor with a new duvet cover! But instead of paying big bucks for a designer spread, save money by making your own. Look for low-priced linens at discount stores and white sales, and buy two flat sheets the same size as your old comforter. Place the right sides of the sheets together, and sew straight lines down three sides. Turn inside out, and attach closures—like snaps, buttons, Velcro, or grommets and ribbon—to the fourth side. Insert your old comforter, and admire your frugillionaire handiwork. You'll sleep a lot better when your bedding doesn't break the bank!

109 Slipcover it!

Instead of buying a new sofa, spruce up your current one with a slipcover! Slipcovers are much less expensive than reupholstery, and help give hand-me-downs a chic makeover. They're available in a variety of colors and styles, to fit couches, recliners, chairs and ottomans. If you're on a tight budget, sew your own, or use inexpensive flat sheets: just tuck, pin and staple to secure. Tie decorative cording around the bottom for a more formal look. Slipcovers can also dress up folding chairs for entertaining, and protect your upholstery from children, pets and other wear and tear.

110 Expand your closet space

From a design perspective, there's nothing worse than stuff without a place—it clutters our homes, our minds and our souls. Pare down what you can, and keep the rest out of sight by expanding your closet space. There's no need to hire a contractor, or buy an expensive armoire; simply stretch a curtain along one wall, or across the corner of a room. Attach a rod or track to the ceiling, and hang with fabric that reaches to the floor. Behind it: set up shelving or milk crates, affix cup hooks to the wall, or keep a rack for hanging clothes. It's a great way to create extra storage space on a tight budget!

111 Light up your life

Good lighting is not only practical; it's a low-cost way to enhance the look of a room. Maximize natural light during the day for a bright, open, airy feel (and a lower electric bill!). For evenings and overcast days, use lamps to create a cozy glow. Purchase them inexpensively at discount retailers, thrift stores, or garage sales. For a custom look: paint the base, and decorate the shade with stencils, pressed flowers, or a pattern of holes. And for countertops, shelving, and closets, pass on the pricey hard-wired fixtures; try budget-friendly, battery-powered lights instead!

112 Decorate with photos

A house adorned with personal photos delights its inhabitants, and their guests! Channel your inner curator, and arrange your pictures like works of art. Group similar themes like ancestors, children, nature, travel or special occasions. Mount them in simple, identical frames, to highlight the images without distracting from them. For a sophisticated, high-art style, scan the photos into your computer, and convert them to black-and-white or sepia tones. Alternatively: select one special image, super-size it, and have it printed on canvas for a wonderful graphic punch.

113 Use illustrations

Don't spring for expensive artwork to jazz up your walls; beautiful illustrations can be had for next to nothing! Print pictures from the internet, or tear them out of old calendars. Vintage books have gorgeous images of birds, landscapes, flowers, botanicals, people, paintings and architecture. Buy them cheaply at secondhand bookstores or yard sales, or borrow them from the library. If you don't want to (or can't) tear out the pages: photocopy the pictures, or use your computer to scan and print them. Cluster similar subjects in matching frames, or hang them from binder clips nailed to the wall.

114 Frame your collections

Use frames and shadow boxes to display small items you've collected. For best results, group similar pieces that vary in size, color or detail: antique buttons, brooches, and keys are good examples. Alternatively, use pressed flowers and leaves, or other gifts of nature; they're absolutely free, and have lovely artistic appeal. Postcards, greeting cards, playbills, matchbooks, and pieces of pretty fabric are also suitable for framing. Vignettes that commemorate special occasions—by combining, for instance, a wedding photo, swatch of gown, and flowers from the bride's bouquet—are particularly charming!

115 Spruce up your kitchen

Don't take on debt to redo your kitchen; spruce it up with some frugillionaire techniques! For example, give cabinets a facelift instead of replacing them. All it takes is a coat of paint, and some new hardware: modern handles and pulls update the style with minimal expense. Or remove cabinet doors altogether for an open-shelf look; it's a great way to show off pretty cups and plates. Use tile from the hardware store to cover an old countertop, or create a chic backsplash. You can even transform your outdated stove, dishwasher or refrigerator with special appliance paint!

116 Showcase functional items

Adorn your kitchen with the things that belong there! Bowls of colorful fruit and vegetables, for instance, look gorgeous on your countertop. Glass jars filled with pasta, beans and nuts, or rows of spices in sleek containers, create a modern gourmet look. Mount pretty plates on the walls, and use ceiling racks to display attractive pots, tools and other implements. For an air of French Provence, hang bundles of lavender and other herbs upside down to dry. Showcase your culinary items with style, and you'll have a beautiful kitchen on a minimal budget!

117 Beautify your bathroom

You don't have to spend big bucks to have a beautiful bathroom! Create a luxurious look for less, with a few simple changes. Paint the walls white, or a light color; it makes a small room look larger, brighter, and airier. You can also use paint to cover unattractive tile (in areas that don't get soaking wet), and to freshen up cabinets (it's cheaper than replacing them). Instead of paying a contractor to expand the bath, create more elbowroom with a curved shower rod. Reduce clutter on shelves and countertops; and accessorize with white towels, fresh flowers and candles for a spa-like ambience!

118 Go large scale

Think big when it comes to décor, and you can make a bold statement on a small budget! Hang a quilt, tapestry or area rug on your wall to create graphic and textural interest. Or staple a large piece of fabric onto a plywood frame, and display like a painting. Alternatively, dip fabric in liquid starch, and smooth directly onto the wall; the starch holds it in place, and it's easy to peel off when you want a change. For a fresh, modern look, paint a large canvas with an abstract color wash. Use stencils to add inspirational words (like "Love," "Dream," or "Believe"), or silhouettes of leaves and flowers.

119 Go modern

Some of the most fashionable homes in the world contain the least amount of stuff! Instead of knick-knacks and accent pieces, they feature sleek lines, neutral colors, and lots of empty space. Fortunately, this super- sophisticated style can be replicated with little expense: simply clear all surfaces of clutter, and keep furniture and accessories to a minimum. As for décor, less is more. Natural items—like a single orchid, cluster of branches, or bowl of pebbles—look particularly beautiful in such a spare setting. With a minimalist modern style, there's no need to buy stuff to "fill" your rooms— making it a very chic way to save money!

120 Choose a theme

When you're decorating a room, choose a theme; it's a great way to create a designer look on a budget! It can be as simple as sticking to a single color, like cool blues, sunny yellows, or fiery reds. Or channel the style of a particular region or culture: Asian, Mediterranean, Parisian and Southwestern are popular choices. Periods in history—such as the Victorian Era, Roaring Twenties or Fabulous Fifties—can also serve as inspiration. A theme provides visual consistency, and can transform a hodgepodge of hand-me-downs and thrift store finds into a smart and stylish room!

121 Rotate your décor

The key to a beautiful room is to keep it well-edited. Don't fill every nook and cranny with tchotchkes, knick-knacks and other décor. Instead, give center stage to a few special items. In traditional Japanese homes, for example, only one or two decorative pieces are displayed at a time. They're the focal point of the room, and are typically chosen according to season. Use the same idea in your own home. Choose a handful of items to exhibit, and store away the extras. Rotate your décor throughout the year. That way, you'll always have a fresh look, without having to buy anything new!

122 Save on cleaning supplies

Don't clean out your bank account in order to clean your home! Use the following tips to get sparkle on a shoestring. Buy cleaning solutions in larger sizes or concentrate form; check the unit price to be sure it's a bargain. Choose an all-purpose or multi-purpose cleaner, rather than numerous specialty products. Select store brands instead of name brands, and buy on sale or with coupons. Use reusable dust cloths and mops; they're cheaper, and more eco-friendly, than disposables. Make cleaning rags out of old clothing and towels. And certainly don't waste money on a housekeeper; scrubbing your floors is good for your soul!

123 Clean with baking soda

Instead of splurging on expensive cleansers, keep your household spic-and-span with baking soda—it's cheap, non-toxic and incredibly versatile. This simple substance deodorizes, polishes and removes stains without harsh chemicals or fragrances. With a little water, it becomes a gently abrasive scouring powder that can be used on pots and pans, tubs and showers, sinks, countertops and other surfaces. Baking soda is also an effective drain cleaner, and can be mixed with Borax to make dishwashing detergent. To neutralize odors: put an open container of it in your refrigerator, sprinkle it on carpet before vacuuming, or add it to your laundry.

124 Clean with vinegar

White vinegar is another natural, inexpensive, household cleaning workhorse! It kills germs and bacteria, and can be used on almost any surface. Fill a spray bottle with equal parts vinegar and water, to make a glass cleaner that doesn't leave streaks. Use the same solution on tubs and tiles; it removes, and inhibits the growth of, mold and mildew. Undiluted white vinegar cleans toilet bowls, stovetops and counters. You can even add half a cup to your laundry to kill bacteria, neutralize odors and soften clothes. The vinegar smell fades as it dries, but you can add a few drops of essential oil (like lavender or citrus) for a more pleasant scent.

125 Clean often

Save money by cleaning regularly and often! Always mop up spills and treat stains immediately; you'll use less cleanser, and eliminate the need for ultra-strong specialty products. Clean kitchen surfaces (including the stovetop) after each meal, and wipe down bathroom sinks and counters before going to bed. Wash dirty dishes right away, and scrape food from plates before setting them in the sink or dishwasher. Keep rooms free of garbage, and vacuum or sweep the floor on a regular basis. When you clean like a frugillionaire—by incorporating a little housekeeping into your daily routine—it costs you less, and doesn't seem so much of a chore!

126 Go shoeless

Take a cue from the Japanese, and remove your shoes at the entrance to your house. Footwear drags in all kinds of dirt and grime, requiring frequent sweeping, mopping and vacuuming. Instead, go shoeless when you're indoors—it's healthier, more sanitary, and saves wear and tear on carpets and flooring. And it's much more comfortable to pad around in socks or slippers! Guests will typically follow suit when they see the family's footwear lined up at the door; for those who don't, keep mats at each entrance to remove dirt. Adopt this simple habit, and you'll have a significantly cleaner house—with much less effort and expense!

Chapter 4

GARDEN

Growing Lush,
Low-Cost Landscapes

---

127 Water only when necessary

When it comes to yard work, a little water conservation goes a long way! Instead of running sprinklers on a regular schedule, water your lawn only when necessary. Grass only needs about one inch of water per week, including rainfall. If your lawn is thirsty, it'll typically show light green patches, and won't spring back when you step on it. Avoid overwatering; it not only wastes money, it promotes the growth of fungus and other lawn disease. Use a kitchen timer to remember to turn off the spigot. And if rain is in the forecast: skip the sprinklers altogether, and let Mother Nature do the work for you!

128 Water wisely

You can lower your water bill—and still have a lovely lawn—with a few smart strategies. First, minimize the amount of water lost to evaporation. Water early in the morning, when temperatures are cooler and winds are calm; and adjust sprinkler heads to emit large drops instead of a fine mist. Second, water longer, but less frequently, to penetrate deeper into roots. Set your lawnmower to cut the grass about 2 ½ to 3 ½ inches high to help keep in the moisture. And third, position sprinklers to avoid wasting water on your sidewalk, street or driveway; better yet, hand-water with a hose.

129 Use drip irrigation

Save big money by installing a drip irrigation system—it uses up to 50 percent less water than conventional sprinklers. Eco-friendly and efficient, drip irrigation delivers the right amount of water to your plants' roots, slowly and steadily, without loss to wind and evaporation. It also eliminates puddles and runoff, and keeps your plants and soil healthier. Flexible pipe and fittings make for easy, low-cost installation; search the internet for do-it-yourself instructions and tutorials. Automate the system with a timer, and you'll have a beautiful yard—with much less work, worry, and water waste!

130 Capture excess water

Think of all the water that runs from your taps while you're waiting for it to warm. Instead of letting it go down the drain, fill some containers to water your plants. Excess water from household chores—like rinsing dishes or boiling pasta—is ideal for use on lawns and non-edible greenery. Capture even larger volumes of water by installing a rain barrel under your gutter system. Purchase a kit from a home improvement or garden center, or rig up your own with instructions from the internet. Use the water collected for landscaping, washing your car, or rinsing dirty tools and boots.

131 Mind your hoses

Don't let leaky hoses drain your bank account! Equip them with automatic shut-off nozzles so that water flows only when needed, rather than continuously. Check them often to see if they're dripping water, and examine couplings and fittings for leaks. And by all means, don't leave running hoses unattended; they can pour out hundreds of gallons of water in only a few hours! When you're finished using a hose, turn it off at the tap, and close the spigot tight. Disconnect hoses from water sources when they won't be used for an extended period of time.

132 Wash cars without wasting water

Save water—and money—by washing your car only when necessary. A good rainstorm may be all that's needed to rinse away dirt, dust and debris! If you can't leave the job to Mother Nature, minimize water waste by using a bucket of soapy water instead of a hose. Be a true frugillionaire, and fill the bucket while waiting for tap water to warm (like when you're doing dishes, or taking a shower); or use water you collected with a rain barrel. Bring out the hose only after you've scrubbed your car and are ready to rinse; make sure it's outfitted with a shut-off nozzle, so you can control the flow and spray.

133 Be frugal with fountains

There's nothing more soothing than a burbling fountain—until your budget springs a leak! Decorative water ornaments can do a number on water and energy bills. When choosing a fountain, look for one that minimizes waste by re-circulating water. Save even more by selecting a model that runs on solar power; it'll cost far less to operate than one that requires an electrical source. If you already have a traditional, non-conserving fountain, you can still enjoy it— just don't leave it running all day and night. Think of it as a special luxury, and turn it on only when you're outside to appreciate it!

134 Do it by hand

Use a broom to sweep sidewalks and driveways; cleaning them with a hose wastes hundreds of gallons of water. The runoff can also send pollution into local bodies of water. Skip the leaf and snow blowers, too; every time you use them, you have to pay for the gas or electricity to power them. They're also expensive to purchase, maintain and repair. Instead, clear leaves, snow and debris manually. Sweeping, raking and shoveling are great workouts for the upper body, and a productive way to burn calories. You may even eliminate the need for a gym membership!

135 Use a push mower

Embrace the retro charm of the old-fashioned push mower; it's good for the environment, as well as your wallet! Push (or reel) mowers are light, quiet and non-polluting. They're cheaper to purchase than gas and electric models, and save you a bundle in operating costs. With a push mower, you won't need to spring for gas, oil, expensive repairs or pricey replacement parts. The only maintenance it needs is periodic blade sharpening, which is easy (and economical) to do yourself. Without the noise and toxic fumes, mowing the lawn is a pleasant activity—and a fantastic workout!

136 Give up your lawn

Save money on water, fertilizers, chemicals and maintenance—by giving up your lawn! There are many attractive alternatives to a manicured, "golf course" look. Wildflowers, native grasses and ground covers provide beautiful, low maintenance landscapes. Mix in areas of rock, gravel or stone tile to accent the vegetation. Alternatively, replace some of your grass with a garden. By growing some of your own fruits and vegetables, you'll reduce your grocery, as well as your lawn care, bill. If you're not ready to eliminate the lawn entirely, try downsizing it; you'll spend less on its upkeep, and have more time to enjoy it!

137 Do your own yard work

Do your own yard work and double your savings: you won't need to pay for a landscaping crew, or a gym membership! Mowing the lawn is a terrific calorie burner. Trimming the hedges and digging in the garden work a variety of muscles, and are much more fun than Nautilus equipment. You'll enjoy being outdoors, and hardly realize you're exercising. So when Mother Nature dumps a load of leaves on your lawn—or a foot of snow on your driveway—don't hire help. Get out your rake or shovel, and be grateful for such a beautiful fitness opportunity!

138 Find free plants in your neighborhood

Instead of paying retail at your local garden store, scout out sources of free plants! Drive around your neighborhood on trash day; you'll often find healthy greenery among the landscaping "debris," and potted plants discarded on the curbside. Contact landscapers, and ask if you can have plants they're tearing out (you'll save them on dumping fees). Make a similar request of local nurseries; they may be willing to give you old stock when clearing their shelves for more vibrant inventory. And don't forget to check community resources, as some towns offer free trees to residents as part of their beautification programs.

139 Find free plants online

Look for free plants along the digital superhighway! Freecyle.com and Craigslist.com are wonderful sources for obtaining greenery at no cost. Browse through the offerings, or post a request for something specific. For best results, focus on what's abundant in your region, instead of seeking out trendy or exotic specimens. Gardeners are a generous lot; when thinning their beds, they love to give extras to fellow enthusiasts. Just be sure your requests are appropriate to the season, and graciously offer to help with digging (or other labor) in return.

140 Grow from seeds

Grow your garden from seeds—they're a fraction of the price of starter plants. Packets usually cost less than a dollar, and you can pick them up for pennies when they're on sale. Don't worry if you lack experience; the seed package is printed with detailed instructions, including the best time to plant, and the amount of water and sunlight required. Start your seeds indoors, a few months before planting season, and transfer the "babies" outside after the last frost. Growing from seed requires some patience; but it's much cheaper, and gives you a wonderful sense of accomplishment!

141 Save seeds

Save seeds from your flowers and vegetables, and you won't need to buy any the following year! Watch carefully as the blooms on your flowers mature and fade; when the petals fall off, you'll see the bulging seedpod. The ideal time to harvest seeds is when they're mature and dry, but haven't yet fallen to the ground. Let collected seeds dry for several days on a flat surface, then store them in a cool, dark, dry place (such as an airtight glass jar, or plastic bag inside the refrigerator). Consult a gardening book, or the internet, for specific advice and techniques. You can even save seeds from store-bought fruits and vegetables!

142 Plant self-seeders

Plant flowers that sow their own seeds—like violas, poppies, larkspur, forget-me-nots, marigolds, zinnias and sunflowers. Your garden will grow fuller each year, with no additional work or expense! The flowers must dry in order for their seeds to mature, so allow late season blooms to go to seed rather than "deadheading" them (removing them when they fade). Self-seeders require virtually no maintenance, and attract beneficial insects to your garden. Just plant them, sit back, and let nature take its course. You'll be rewarded with beautiful new blooms year after year—absolutely free!

143 Grow from cuttings

Expand your garden at no cost—by growing new plants from ones you already have! With a pair of pruning shears, take cuttings from your favorite specimens. Root them in water, or a small pot of soil (consult gardening books or websites for plant-specific instructions). Keep cuttings warm, moist and out of direct sunlight; you can use plastic bags to create a high-humidity, greenhouse-like environment. Once they're rooted, they can be transplanted into the garden. For more variety, swap cuttings with friends, neighbors and other gardeners!

144 Invest in perennials

Garden like a frugillionaire: invest in perennials, instead of splurging on annuals. Annual plants bloom for just a single season, giving a short-lived burst of color to your yard. Perennials, on the other hand, continue to flower year after year. Even better, they multiply over time: individual plants can be divided about every three years. It's a wonderful way to fill other areas of your yard, without spending a dime. Trade extras with friends and neighbors to create a lush, varied garden at minimal cost. Perennials may be a bit more expensive upfront—but they pay beautiful dividends down the road!

145 Know your zone

Select plants appropriate to your area's "zone;" they'll have a much better chance of surviving the winter. The Hardiness Zone Map, published by the United States Department of Agriculture, divides North America into eleven climate zones based on average annual minimum temperatures. Find your region on the map, and make note of the zone in which it falls. When planning your garden, read plant tags and seed packets to see if they're suited to your climate. Knowing your zone—and considering other factors like rainfall, wind, heat and humidity—will save you the money, and frustration, of trying to grow a palm tree in Minnesota!

146 Choose native plants

Choose plants that are native to your area; they're hardier than exotic species, and much less expensive to maintain. Native plants thrive on natural rainfall, and are able to withstand regional temperature extremes; once established, they require no watering or fertilizing. Furthermore, they're usually insect- and disease-resistant, so you'll have little need for pricey pest control products. Incorporating these low-maintenance, drought-tolerant plants into your yard is called xeriscaping. It's an eco-friendly (and financially-savvy) way to landscape!

147 Use recycled containers to start seeds

When growing plants from seeds, you'll need small containers to get them started. But don't buy them from the garden store—look around your house! It's a wonderful opportunity to recycle egg cartons, margarine tubs, soda bottles and yogurt cups. Wash them thoroughly, and sanitize with a solution of bleach and water. Make drainage holes, fill with soil and place on a waterproof tray—old cookie sheets or "disposable" baking pans work nicely. You can even craft little pots from old toilet paper rolls; just cut in half, then fold in the ends to make the bottom (one roll will make two pots).

148 Use recycled containers to hold plants

Don't pay big bucks for fancy pots and planters! Anything that can hold dirt and drain water — like plastic buckets, milk jugs, coffee cans, colanders, baskets, boxes or old boots — makes a fine home for your plants. Drive through your neighborhood on trash day to score some freebies. Or contact landscaping companies and public works departments; they usually have lots of empty containers after major plantings. Try Freecycle.com, Craigslist.com, thrift shops, garage sales and discount stores as well. Remember, your pots don't have to be fashionable; it's what's growing inside them that counts!

149 Fertilize with grass clippings

The next time you mow, let the grass clippings fall as they may! They're a rich source of nitrogen and other nutrients for your lawn. For best results: mow with a sharp blade when the grass is dry, and set the blade height to produce clippings of less than an inch. You can also bag clippings for use in your garden; they prevent weed growth, keep in moisture, and supply the soil with nutrients as they decompose. Grass clippings are a wonderful organic alternative to store-bought fertilizers, and promote the healthy growth of your lawn, your plants and your bank account!

150 Fertilize with compost

Save money on fertilizer by composting! Compost is a dark, crumbly substance formed by the decomposition of vegetable matter and plant waste. It enriches garden soil by retaining moisture, and harboring beneficial bacteria and earthworms. You can make your own compost from leaves, twigs, cuttings, grass clippings, pine needles and other yard "waste," as well as kitchen scraps like vegetable matter, coffee grounds and eggshells. See the internet for instructions on how to layer and stir the materials. Composting is the frugillionaire way to fertilize: it keeps trash out of the landfill, and money in your pocket!

151 Make your own mulch

Mulch is a blanket of material—organic or inorganic that protects the soil around plants and trees. It deters the growth of weeds, prevents erosion, and provides nutrients for plants as it breaks down. It also shields soil from the wind and sun, reducing evaporation and retaining moisture. Save money by making your own mulch, instead of buying it from garden centers. Shredded leaves, grass, bark, sticks, pine needles and wood chips are all effective mulching materials. Consult gardening books or websites to learn which substances are best for your particular plants.

152 Use natural pest control

Forget the chemicals, and use natural pest control in your garden. Homemade sprays that combine dishwashing liquid with other ingredients—like vegetable oil, cayenne pepper or garlic—are effective insect repellants. Search the internet for formulas appropriate to your needs. The best defense against pests, however, is a good offense. In your garden, include plants that host beneficial bugs; these, in turn, will prey on pests. For example, plant marigolds among your vegetables; they'll attract insects that eat aphids. It's much less expensive (and safer for the environment) than buying pesticides!

153 Hardscape with recycled materials

Hardscaping doesn't have to cost a fortune! Seek out materials to recycle and reuse for paths, walkways, walls, borders, fences and arbors. Comb your neighborhood (or search Freecycle.com and Craigslist.com) for old bricks, concrete blocks, pavers, river rocks and railroad ties; they're often discarded when homeowners redo their landscaping. With a little creativity, the possibilities are endless: you can make greenhouses from old windows, build trellises from wood and wire, and craft benches from discarded doors. Broken plates, pots and tiles make lovely decorations, especially when arranged into artful mosaics!

154 Go solar

Decorative lighting adds beauty, charm and romance to your outdoor space. You may be less enchanted, however, when you see your electric bill! Save energy, and money, by replacing traditional illumination with solar powered lights. They're inexpensive and easy to install, and can be used to line pathways, border patios, and accent your garden. Solar powered lights require no wiring: the sun charges their batteries during the day, and darkness sensors switch them on at night. You'll never have to remember to turn them on or off—making them low-maintenance, as well as cost-effective!

155 Get to know gardeners

Make friends with other gardeners; they'll provide you with more information about local growing conditions, and native varieties, than you'll ever find in books! They'll also be happy to swap seeds, cuttings and plants with you, and will likely provide you with plenty of greenery when thinning out their beds. Consider teaming up to make joint orders from catalogs—you'll get bulk discounts and save on shipping charges. Wondering how to find fellow green thumbs? Join a gardening club, get a plot in your community garden, or simply strike up a conversation with a plant-loving neighbor!

156 Rent, share and borrow tools

You don't need a garage full of tools to be a great gardener! It's very satisfying—and far less expensive—to work with basic hand implements. All it takes to get started is a shovel, hoe, fork, rake, spade, hose and watering can. As your garden grows, you may find need for a more specialized item; if it's something you won't use often, rent or borrow instead of buying it. Alternatively, organize a tool share in your neighborhood, and use the funds collected from members to purchase a shared set of equipment. It'll save everyone money, and encourage a wonderful sense of community and camaraderie!

157 Buy used tools

Garden tools don't stay shiny and new for long; so why pay extra to buy them that way? Used tools are often great values, as well-made ones can last through generations; look for them at thrift stores, auctions, and garage or estate sales. Elderly or affluent communities—where gardening is a common hobby—can be a treasure trove of secondhand equipment. It's also worthwhile to browse the listings on Freecycle.com and Craigslist.com; many people give away yard and garden supplies when they move. And keep your eyes peeled on trash day—you may find some wonderful freebies on the curbside!

158 Care for your tools

Save money by properly caring for garden tools; with good maintenance, you may never need to buy replacements! Make it a habit to clean your tools after every use. A simple rinsing will wash away dirt, while soap can be added to remove fertilizer chemicals. Dry thoroughly with a towel, and wipe metal parts with an oily rag, to prevent rust; if any develops, remove it immediately with steel wool or a wire brush. Keep wooden handles smooth by sanding and rubbing with linseed oil. Sharpen tools regularly with a hand file or sharpening stone to ensure their maximum performance.

159 Shop end-of-season sales

For terrific savings on lawn and garden supplies, shop end-of-season sales at nurseries, garden centers, supermarkets and discount stores. Retailers must clear out the current season's stock to make room for the next, so they slash prices to move merchandise off the shelves. It's a great opportunity to get plants, trees, seeds, tools and other landscaping materials at deep discounts. You'll also find bargains on perennials throughout the summer, as stores replace plants past their peak with a fresh batch. You may have to wait another year for the blooms, but your patience will be duly rewarded!

160 Enjoy public parks

If you're a plant lover—but short on time, money or yard space—get your greenery fix at the local park! Public parks are a wonderful way to enjoy the gifts of Mother Nature, without lifting a finger or spending a dime. Landscape crews keep them in tip-top shape, and full of seasonal blooms, for your viewing pleasure. It'd be impossible to match the grand scale, and rich variety, of such public spaces in your backyard; you might as well leave it to the experts, and enjoy the fruits of their labor like a frugillionaire! For more exotic specimens and creative displays, visit your local horticultural gardens.

161 Use community resources

Take advantage of agricultural resources offered by your community. Some municipalities give out free mulch and compost as part of recycling programs, while others hold workshops to provide information on native plants and local growing conditions. Residents can obtain plots in community gardens, and in some towns, may even be able to score some free trees! Furthermore, each state has an office of the nationwide Cooperative Extension System. This program offers soil testing and other services; supplies information on frost dates, diseases and pests; and has trained volunteers available to answer gardening questions.

Chapter 5

FASHION

Dressing to the Nines
on Next to Nothing

---

162 Never pay retail

Don't pay full price for department store clothing; it's certain to be on sale in the near future! Instead, play the waiting game: watch for advertisements and coupons, and then congratulate yourself when you save 30 percent on that new sweater. Alternatively, check the racks at stores like Ross, Marshalls and TJ Maxx—you'll find department store brands at deep discounts. And if you see something on sale for which you recently paid a higher price, take that receipt to customer service: many stores will refund the difference within a certain time period.

163 Buy vintage

For beautiful clothes that are easy on the budget, think vintage! Consignment shops and vintage clothing stores are a treasure trove of finely tailored, classic pieces. Keep an eye out for items made in Italy, France, England and the USA; the fabric, construction and finishing is often of a higher quality than what you'll find in today's department stores. Back in their day, these clothes were considered investments and made to last years (if not decades). If you have a weakness for high-end labels, shopping vintage will save you a considerable amount of money; it's much more affordable to be the *second* owner of a designer piece!

164 Shop eBay

Many people have perfectly good clothes in their closets they never wear; and they're yours for the bidding on eBay.com! Online auctions are a great source of gently-used name brand clothing. Some pieces have never even been worn; look for "NWT," which means "New with tags." Offerings number in the thousands; narrow your search by brand, color, size or clothing type to save time. There's no dressing room, so it helps to be familiar with the sizing of your favorite labels. Before you bid, ask the seller for specific measurements— and find out whether you can return the item if it doesn't fit.

165 Organize a fashion swap

Get together with some frugillionaire friends for a clothing swap! Have everyone bring a few items—clothes, handbags, and other accessories—they're no longer wearing. Set up a little "boutique" in the corner of your living room, and display the goods on a table, shelf or portable clothes rack. Mix cocktails, serve hors d'oeuvres, and let everyone do some "shopping." At the end of the night, stage a fashion show: clear a path in the center of the room, put on some music, and have each person walk the runway to show off their new finds!

166 Mix and match colors

Buy clothes in colors that mix and match, and stretch your fashion dollars further. Choose a base like black, gray, khaki or brown for wardrobe staples; these shades give you the most mileage out of pants, skirts, suits and shoes. Add color with shirts, sweaters, ties, scarves and accessories. Keep to a certain color palette—like pastels, primaries, jewel or earth tones—for maximum versatility. Avoid hues that don't go with anything else in your closet. It doesn't matter if that chartreuse top is on sale; it's not a good value if you have nothing to wear it with!

167 Dress it up, dress it down

The best values in your wardrobe aren't the least expensive pieces, but the most versatile. When you're considering a clothing purchase, think about how often you'll be able to wear it. Can that sweater go from work to dinner, and also look great with jeans on the weekend? If so, it earns a place in your closet! Skip the sequins and sweatshirts, and any other items that'll be "too dressy" or "too casual" most of the time. Instead, buy pieces you can dress up or dress down, depending on the occasion. The more outfits you can make from a few garments, the more money you'll save!

168 Buy classic

Buy simple, classic clothing, and you'll always be in style. A basic black skirt, khaki trouser, white shirt or wool coat can serve as a wardrobe staple for years. When you stick to items that stay in fashion, you eliminate the need to shop each season—thereby saving a substantial amount of cash. Furthermore, you'll never run the risk of looking dated, or being caught in last year's "must have." Think about it: you could wear the same black pants to work multiple times a week and no one would notice; but try that with a ruffled, leopard-print top, and you'll likely raise some eyebrows!

169 Don't be a fashion victim

One season skinny pants are in fashion, and the next it's wide-leg trousers; mini-skirts, then maxi-skirts; empire waists, then drop waists. And of course, there's always the "It" bag and the "It" shoe—seen on a handful of "It" girls and out of style ten minutes later. Fashion trends move at the speed of light; you'd go broke—or at least deep into debt—trying to keep up with them. Instead, ignore the fashion media, and invest in pieces that flatter you and fit your lifestyle. Don't spend a hard-earned paycheck on something that'll be "out" (and that you'll feel ridiculous wearing!) in just a few months.

170 Accessorize

Make the most of a limited wardrobe by adding accessories. Take a cue from fashionable Parisians, and use chic accents—like a strand of pearls, colorful bag or chunky bracelet—to liven up simple, classic clothes. Why drop $200 on a new outfit, when you can spice up an old one with a $20 scarf? Stick to basic silhouettes and neutrals for your "core" wardrobe, and choose handbags, scarves, belts and jewelry to add color and pizzazz. Changing your accessories is a great way to update your look—and show your sense of style—without blowing your budget!

171 Get a good fit

Buy clothes that fit, and you'll save a ton of money on tailoring. Not all labels are flattering to all body types: some cater to the curvy, while others are built for boyish figures. Find the brands that fit you best, and you'll feel comfortable and confident in your clothes. Don't be tempted by items that *almost* fit, even if they're on sale; the cost of alterations can add a pretty penny to the purchase price. And by all means, don't buy clothes in smaller sizes as an inspiration to diet; reward yourself with something new *after* you've dropped the pounds!

172 Learn what flatters you

Learn which colors and silhouettes flatter you, and you'll avoid wasting money on wardrobe "mistakes." Determine if you look best in fitted or flowing clothes; straight lines or soft curves; crew, ballet, or v-shaped necklines. Consider whether sleeveless, short-sleeve or ¾-sleeve tops flatter your arms, and if it's better to show your legs or hide them. Think about which colors complement your skin tone, and which ones wash it out. Then shop accordingly: purchase pieces that play up your assets, and avoid those that accentuate flaws. No matter how fashionable an item, it's not a good buy if it's wrong for *you*!

173 Shop out of season

Save a bundle by shopping for sweaters in June, and bathing suits in October! When retailers need floor space for new inventory, they offer last season's merchandise at deep discounts. Pieces that sold for a premium a few months ago are suddenly in the bargain bin—marked down 50 percent or more. Buy them now, and squirrel them away for next year. For best results, focus on classic clothing, and avoid trendy items that'll look outdated by the time you wear them. This frugillionaire technique is a great way to build a fabulous wardrobe at rock bottom prices!

174 Don't buy it *because* it's on sale

Just because something's on sale, doesn't mean it's a bargain! Clothes are a good value only if you wear them often. If you would have never considered that purple velvet jacket at full price, don't buy it at half. Chances are, it'll sit in your closet, unloved and unworn, for years to come. If you spend $100 on a pair of pants, and wear them once a week for two years, that's only $1 per wear—a terrific value! On the other hand, that fuchsia mini-skirt you bought on sale for $49—and wore only once—is a waste of money. Better to have a few wardrobe staples, than a closet full of barely-used, bargain-basement duds.

175 Don't buy "wish" clothes

Resist the temptation to shop for your "fantasy" self—the one who attends cocktail parties, hits the gym each morning, or is ten pounds thinner. Fancy dresses, exercise wear and skinny clothes won't transform you into a different person; they'll just sit there, unworn, reminding you of what you are *not*. Skip the "wish" clothes, and celebrate your real self instead: choose outfits that make you feel comfortable, and suit your current lifestyle. Purchase clothes in the size you wear *now*; get the cute yoga pants *after* you sign up for class; and buy the ball gown when the black tie invitation's in hand!

176 Remember the 80/20 rule

According to the 80/20 rule (otherwise known as the Pareto principle), we wear 20% of our wardrobe 80% of the time. That means the majority of our clothes languish in our closets, rarely worn. We could have put that money in the bank, and hardly noticed a difference getting dressed in the morning! Think about which items constitute your 20%: it'll likely include that gray suit, black skirt, white blouse or navy sweater you wear once a week. The next time you're contemplating a purchase, consider if the item will be in your "favorite 20" or "unworn 80." Invest in the former—and skip the latter—for big savings!

177 Shop your closet

Instead of going to the mall, have a shopping spree inside your own closet. You likely have clothes in there that haven't seen the light of day for months (or even years!). Take everything out and try it on—you'll find at least one or two items to bring back into regular rotation. Perhaps you've lost a few pounds, and something that didn't fit before is suddenly just right. Or maybe your wide-leg pants or bohemian top is back in fashion this season. Don't buy anything new until you've shopped what you already own; you may be able to put together a "new" look without spending a dime!

178 Set limits

Save money by setting limits on the number of clothes you own. If your closet is already stuffed, don't buy anything new until something wears out. Or, if you tend to buy too many items of the same type—like skirts, shoes, or blouses—cap your collection at a certain number. Don't bring home that eleventh pair of shoes, for example, until it's time to replace one of the other ten. Your closet, and your wallet, will breathe much easier! Price limits are another option: decide that you'll never spend more than a set amount (say $100) on a single item of clothing, and don't try on anything that's out of your "budget."

179 Make a clothing inventory

Before you buy another piece of clothing, make an inventory of what you have. Empty the entire contents of your closet, and write down each item as you put it back. Organize your list into categories—so you can see just how many shirts, sweaters, pants and shoes you actually own. It's easy to forget about purchases once you tuck them away—and shocking to discover you have twenty-three blouses, or thirty pairs of shoes! Making an inventory is a great way to realize you *do* have enough. Take the list with you when shopping, and you'll be much less likely to spend hard-earned cash on a twenty-fourth blouse!

180 Simplify your shoes

Kick your shoe-buying habit, and add hundreds (if not thousands) of dollars to your bottom line. From now on, purchase only footwear that's versatile; make it *earn* a place in your closet by working with a variety of outfits. Classic black pumps, for example, stretch your shoe dollar much further than lime-green stilettos. Resist the urge to splurge on impractical, uncomfortable or single-occasion shoes, no matter how cute or sexy they may be. Stick to neutral colors and basic styles—like flat, pump, boot, sandal, and dressy heel—and strut to the bank with your savings!

181 Return it

Sometimes what looks great in the dressing room—in flattering light and "skinny" mirrors—has much less appeal after you bring it home. You don't have to live with your mistakes! If you bought the item recently, and haven't worn it, return it. Most stores let you bring back unworn clothing for a reasonable time period after its purchase (usually from 30 to 90 days). Just be sure to keep your receipts; otherwise, you'll have to accept the lowest markdown price. And don't cut tags off new clothing until you first wear it—you may change your mind in the meantime.

182 Get cash for your cast-offs

If you have clothes you don't wear lurking in your closet, unload them for cash! Name brand and designer pieces sell particularly well through online auctions like eBay.com. Snap photos and set your starting price, then sit back and watch the bids roll in! Alternatively, take gently worn, stain-free garments to a consignment shop. They'll put your clothes on their racks for a certain time period—usually 30, 60 or 90 days—and you'll receive a percentage of the purchase price for any that sell. Donate the leftovers to charity, and take the write-off on your taxes.

183 Wash and wear

Beware of clothes that require professional dry cleaning; the cost of laundering them over several years can exceed the purchase price! Avoid this extra expense by purchasing items you can put in the washing machine. If you already own "dry clean only" garments, you may be able to wash them by hand; consult the internet for fabric-specific instructions. Alternatively, obtain a home dry cleaning kit consisting of cleaning sheets and dryer-safe plastic bags. It may not eliminate trips to the dry cleaner, but can certainly reduce their frequency.

184 Do less laundry

Do less laundry! Who doesn't like the sound of that? It's a favorite frugillionaire strategy for saving time, energy and money. Many clothes don't need to be washed after each wear; simply air them out by hanging on a chair, clothes rack, or back of a door. There's no sense in laundering something that isn't actually dirty! Use the "sniff test," or presence of stains, to determine when it's time for a cleaning. You'll not only slash your water and energy bills by running the washer and dryer less often; you'll also prolong the life of your clothes, and have less need to shop for replacements.

185 Give your clothes some TLC

Make your clothes last longer by taking good care of them. One of the best ways to save money is by getting the most wear possible out of clothes you already own. Sometimes it's just a matter of common sense: don't wear your silk blouse or suede shoes if you know it's going to rain, and don't sport those new white pants at your kid's soccer game. A little preventative maintenance also goes a long way: fix little tears before they become big ones, and treat stains before they turn stubborn. A little planning, mending and TLC can preserve your wardrobe for years!

186 Learn to mend

Our great-grandparents would have never discarded a sock with a hole, or a shirt with a missing button. Such items went straight into the mending pile! Follow their lead, and learn to make these small repairs; you'll extend the life of your clothes, and reduce the need to replace them. You don't even need a sewing machine; a simple needle and thread will do. Borrow a basic sewing book from the library, ask someone handy for help, or search the internet for easy tutorials on hemming garments, replacing buttons and fixing tears. Invite over some other frugillionaires, and have an old-fashioned mending party!

187 Learn to sew

If you have the time and interest, you can save a small fortune by making your own clothes. Sewing isn't rocket science; a hundred years ago, almost every woman knew how to do it. It's something of a lost art in this era of mass production, but with practice and perseverance, you can begin sewing basic garments in short order. Pick up a book on sewing techniques, and purchase an inexpensive machine to get started (find bargains on Craigslist.com and in the classifieds). For your first projects, use "Easy" patterns that are specially designed for beginners; they're a great way to build skills and confidence before tackling more complicated styles.

188 Get shoes repaired

An old pair of shoes is like a good friend—a comfortable, familiar part of your daily life. Instead of throwing them away when they start to wear thin, take them to the repair shop and have them resoled. By the same token, don't toss pumps if the heel caps fall off; they can be replaced for as little as $5. Such small, inexpensive fixes save big bucks over buying brand new pairs. Further extend the life of your footwear with a little preventative maintenance. Polish shoes regularly to protect and condition the leather; and make it a habit to clean off dirt, and buff out scuffmarks, before putting them away.

189 Rent formalwear

It's common for men to rent tuxedos; but did you know women can rent formalwear as well? It's much more practical than spending hundreds (or even thousands) of dollars on a gown you'll wear only once. Not only will you save on the purchase price, you'll avoid the cost and hassle of cleaning, maintaining and storing such a fragile garment. And unlike rental cars, there's no logo on the derriere to announce that you're borrowing it! Rental services offer a variety of formal attire, including designer suits, cocktail dresses, prom dresses and bridal gowns—so you can be the belle of the ball, without breaking the bank!

190 Wash clothes in cold

For big savings, wash clothes in cold water. Heating the water accounts for most of the energy consumed while washing; eliminate the heat, and you'll slash your energy bills. The cold setting is sufficient for all but the dirtiest loads of laundry. It also keeps your clothes looking new longer, as high temperatures can shrink fabrics and fade colors. Use a cold-water detergent, and pre-treat stains, for best results. Save even more by replacing your old washer with an ENERGY STAR model—they use about 50 percent less water and energy than standard machines.

191 Air-dry clothes

Air-dry your laundry; it's super-easy, eco-friendly, and absolutely free! Hanging a clothesline is no more a chore than loading the dryer, and it has a retro charm that makes you want to sit on the porch, chat with your neighbors and sip lemonade. What's more, air-drying clothes keeps them in better shape; the rough and tumble of machines can cause snagging, fraying, shrinking and wearing of seams. It also reduces wrinkles, and eliminates static cling. If the weather's uncooperative, don't despair; retractable clotheslines and drying racks are available for indoor use.

192 Fake the family jewels

You don't have to spend a fortune to get a little bling! Diamond simulants like cubic zirconia give you a lot of flash for your cash. Lab-created rubies, sapphires and emeralds are chemically identical to their natural counterparts, but significantly less expensive. Faux pearls add a touch of elegance to any outfit, and are almost impossible to distinguish from real ones by sight. In fact, they were favorites of both Jackie Onassis and Coco Chanel, two of the most stylish women of the twentieth century. So feel free to fake the family jewels; you'll save serious money, and most people will be none the wiser!

193 Go for silver instead of gold

If you have a thing for baubles and bangles, buy silver jewelry instead of gold—it's a fraction of the price. The metal's low cost gives designers and artisans the freedom to be creative, without fear of making a costly mistake—making silver pieces not only affordable, but often quite unique and stylish. Look for a "925" stamp to make sure an item is sterling (92.5 percent pure) silver. To prevent tarnish, store silver jewelry out of direct sunlight, in small cloth pouches or ziplock bags. Use a chemical solution or polishing cloth to remove any discoloration that develops.

Chapter 6

BEAUTY

Staying Gorgeous
on a Budget

---

194 Wear sunscreen every day

Apply sunscreen every day of the year—it's the single most frugal, and effective, beauty treatment available. UVA and UVB rays from sunlight cause the majority of premature skin aging, including wrinkles and brown spots. They break down collagen, create free radicals, and obstruct the skin's ability to repair itself naturally. Protect yourself against such damage by using a basic sunscreen, or SPF moisturizer, on a daily basis. This simple habit will save you substantial money in the long run—by eliminating the need for expensive creams, potions and other anti-aging treatments!

195 Relax!

Stress avoidance is an essential part of a frugillionaire's beauty regimen. Stress is pro-inflammatory and pro-aging: it can aggravate the skin, induce flare-ups of acne and rosacea, and cause hair loss and brittle nails. It's also responsible for a host of serious health problems. Relieve stress by avoiding the tendency to over-schedule, reducing unrealistic expectations of yourself and others, and getting plenty of exercise and rest. If you approach each day with a laid-back, positive attitude, you'll save a fortune on beauty and medical treatments!

196 Quit smoking

Quit smoking! Not only will you eliminate the expense of cigarettes, you'll reap enormous health and beauty benefits. Smoking causes bad breath, stained teeth and premature wrinkling. Stop now, and you'll be rewarded with smoother skin, fresher breath and a whiter smile. You'll also avoid a slew of medical problems and their associated costs. Your risk of heart attack drops within twenty-four hours of cessation, and your blood flow and breathing improve within days. In a few years, your risk of stroke and coronary heart disease falls to that of a nonsmoker. Kick the habit ASAP—you'll save your looks, your money, and possibly your life!

197 Exercise outdoors

Ditch the expensive gym membership—especially if you don't use it regularly—and exercise in the great outdoors. Mother Nature offers a variety of aerobic activities that are infinitely more scenic, interesting and frugal than a fitness club. Head outside, and run, walk, hike, bike, skate or row your way to fabulous health! You'll lose weight, rather than money; and the fresh air will do wonders for both your physical and mental welfare. Join an organized activity—such as a running club or softball team—for an added sense of camaraderie and motivation!

198 Take a daily walk

Take a brisk, 30-minute walk every day; it's a great way to stay fit without splurging on health clubs and diet pills. Studies show that a daily walk has tremendous benefits for your body: it helps relieve stress, manage weight, and control blood pressure. It also builds bone and muscle strength, lessens arthritis pain, and decreases the risk of heart attack and stroke. Furthermore, the fresh air and physical activity will improve your sleep, and increase your overall sense of well-being. It's amazing how such a simple, enjoyable routine can alleviate so many ailments—and make you feel like a million bucks!

199 Don't believe in magic

Cosmetic companies profit by selling us hope in a bottle. They spend millions each year hawking lotions to smooth out our wrinkles, erase our age spots, and make us look twenty years younger; and potions that promise thicker hair, fuller lips and longer lashes. Such claims, however, are often unsubstantiated. When you hand over hard-earned money for a tiny jar of miracle goop, no results are guaranteed. (If the stuff really worked, we'd *all* look like supermodels!) Better to save the cash, and opt for proven health and beauty boosters: like sunscreen, exercise, a healthy diet, plenty of water, and a good night's sleep!

200 Shop the drugstore's beauty aisle

The next time you need a beauty fix, skip the mall and head to the drugstore! High prices don't always mean high quality. When you purchase designer cosmetics, you're paying for pretty bottles, fancy packaging and pricey ad campaigns—not necessarily results. In fact, some drugstore items regularly outperform their department store counterparts in consumer studies. Don't be afraid to mix things up: if you're reluctant to give up your high-end foundation, balance your budget with an inexpensive blush or eyeshadow. Give bargain brands a chance, and you'll be gorgeous *and* rich!

201 Use half a glob

Use half the amount of lotions and potions—and get double the bang for your beauty buck! Stretch shampoo, conditioner, body wash, toothpaste, moisturizer and wrinkle creams by doing the job with a smaller glob. You'll likely find that lesser amounts are equally effective. It's also a good idea to skip the super-size bottles, unless the savings are significant; they're harder to control, and encourage more generous use. Another way to extend high-end creams, perfumes and cosmetics is to use them every other day, alternating with a less expensive drugstore brand.

202 Do your own manicures and pedicures

If we can hold down demanding jobs, keep our households running smoothly, take care of the kids, do home repairs, and whip up delicious meals—we're certainly capable of doing our own manicures and pedicures! In fact, waiting for your nails to dry is a great opportunity for a little relaxation. Don't let perfectionism deter you; just stay between the lines and you'll be fine. Unless you're a hand or foot model, no one will notice a few minor flubs. For even more fun, have friends over for a "Manis and Pedis" party, where you share your favorite polishes and do each other's nails!

203 Have a spa day at home

A day at the spa is a wonderful experience, but it can be very expensive! Fortunately, much of what we love about it—the products, ambience, and chance to relax—can be replicated at home for little to no cost. Schedule some time for yourself, and set the atmosphere with candlelight and soothing music. Indulge in a long bubble bath, give yourself a manicure and pedicure, and whip up a homemade facial. You can find recipes on the internet for avocado, oatmeal and yogurt masks; citrus and chamomile astringents; and salt, sugar, and walnut scrubs. A "spa day" is even more relaxing when you don't have to pay for it!

204 Go to beauty school

If you have a simple hairdo, or just need a trim, skip the salon and go to beauty school! Student stylists need practice, so training schools offer free (or low-cost) cuts to willing patrons. Don't be nervous: instructors are usually present, and students take care to do a good job—they're being graded, after all! Relax, be gracious, and leave a tip; treat them as professionals, and you'll get quality service in return. Beauty academies also give inexpensive manicures, pedicures, facials and other treatments—providing a great way to get a spa experience on the cheap!

205 Get a free makeover

If you're planning a big night out—or just want to indulge a little—get a free makeover! Cosmetic counters commonly offer them as a way of marketing their line. There's usually no obligation to purchase the products; if there is, it should be disclosed beforehand. Try to work with a makeup artist rather than a sales associate: they're more experienced, and are usually paid an hourly rate instead of a commission (meaning less pressure for you to buy!). Chat with the artist while they're working their magic; you'll pick up some great tips you can use at home.

206 Exfoliate with a washcloth

Instead of splurging on facial scrubs and salon treatments, exfoliate with a dry washcloth! The rough texture sloughs off dead skin cells, leaving you with a fresh, healthy glow. If your skin is dry or sensitive, be gentle: lightly pat the washcloth on your face in small circles. For normal skin, you can exert a little more pressure, and use upward strokes to lift off dead skin patches. Removing old, damaged cells evens out skin tone and stimulates cellular renewal. You'll gain a radiant, more youthful complexion—the frugillionaire way!

207 Beautify with baking soda

Baking soda provides another inexpensive and effective way to exfoliate skin. Its mildly abrasive texture removes dead skin cells, without the irritating effects of harsh chemicals. Sprinkle some into your hand, then add enough water to make a paste. With your fingertips, rub the mixture gently onto your skin in a circular motion. Rinse with water, and admire your new radiance! Baking soda is a beauty workhorse: it can be used for tooth brushing, hand cleansing, foot soaking, hair care, and even as a deodorant. You can also add it to your bath to soften skin, or soothe itching and irritation.

208 Remove makeup with baby wipes

Don't waste money on pricey makeup removers; baby wipes do a fine job, at a fraction of the cost! They can handle big messes, yet are gentle enough for delicate skin—making them perfect for cleaning your face. In fact, they're a favorite of models, movie stars and television anchors, who regularly use them to take off heavy stage makeup. For best results, buy hypoallergenic, unscented wipes; they contain only water, aloe and vitamin E, with no harsh ingredients to irritate skin. If you find them to be larger than needed, cut them in half; you'll reduce waste and stretch your dollar further!

209 Wash your face with honey

Be sweet to your skin, and give your face a honey wash once or twice a week! Honey is antibacterial by nature, and renowned for its healing properties. It tightens pores and moisturizes skin, and is believed to help treat and control acne. Wet your face with warm water, massage with a tablespoon of raw, unprocessed honey, and rinse well. Or, apply the honey as a mask: spread a thin layer over your face, and let it sit 15-20 minutes before washing it off. Your skin will be softer and smoother, without the expense of acne washes and miracle creams!

210 Use witch hazel as a toner

Witch hazel is a great budget alternative to cosmetic counter toners. It's natural, gentle and alcohol-free, and won't dry out skin like chemical-based formulas. Place a small amount on a cotton ball or cosmetic round, and wipe across your face after washing. It refreshes your skin, while removing excess oils, impurities and dead cells. It can also be used to treat bruises, swelling and inflammation. Look for witch hazel in the skin care or first aid section of pharmacies and grocery stores. It doesn't look fancy, but it tones your skin for a song!

211 Steam your face

Give yourself a warm steam facial—it unclogs pores and moisturizes skin. First, clean your face thoroughly, and tie back your hair. Then boil a pot of water, and remove it from the heat. Make a tent over your head with a towel, and position your face about 12 inches above the bowl. Close your eyes and relax for 5-10 minutes while the steam works its magic. The deep cleaning removes dirt and bacteria, and helps clear up pimples and blemishes. For a more luxurious experience, add herbs such as peppermint, lavender or chamomile to the boiled water.

212 Enjoy an oatmeal facial

Oatmeal makes a frugal, yet fabulous, facial! It has a wonderful calming effect on the skin, reducing irritation and inflammation. Its polymers and proteins also fight dryness, while helping to build up your skin's natural defenses. Incorporate it into your beauty regimen by using it as a mask: simply mix dry oatmeal and water into a paste and spread it on your face. Let it dry, then rinse with warm water. It removes dirt, oil and impurities, and restores your skin's moisture balance. Use once a week for best results— and get a beautiful complexion on a budget!

213 Fight blemishes with tea tree oil

No matter how well we treat our skin, we all fall victim to the occasional pimple. Acne creams and medications can be quite costly, however, and their harsh ingredients can further irritate skin. Try tea tree oil instead—it's an inexpensive, natural antiseptic that kills bacteria without chemicals. Tea tree oil effectively relieves minor skin irritations, and clears up blemishes; just dab a small amount on the inflamed spot, in the morning and at night. Its antibacterial and anti-fungal properties also make it an effective treatment for foot odor and bad breath.

214 Give hands and feet a spa treatment

Lavish your hands and feet with a luxurious, moisturizing treatment—without going to the spa! The next time you wash dishes, coat your hands with a thick layer of lotion and don a pair of latex gloves. The gloves retain the heat, and the warmth of the water helps the lotion absorb into your skin. By the time your sink is clear, your hands will be soft and silky smooth! Give your feet a similar treat: before bed, spread lotion or petroleum jelly over them and cover with socks. Leave on for the night, and wake up the next morning with fabulous feet!

215 Use olive oil all over

Olive oil is another low-cost, natural substance with myriad beauty benefits! Soak your fingers in a warm bowl of it to soften cuticles and strengthen nails. Massage onto elbows and knees to smooth away rough patches. Add to your bath to soften skin, and dab a drop on dry or chapped lips. Olive oil is also an effective facial moisturizer, makeup remover and hair conditioner—and can even be used in place of shaving cream! Be sure to buy the "extra virgin" variety, as the "pure" and "light" types are lesser grade oils that have been chemically processed.

216 Buy multi-tasking products

Stretch your beauty bucks with multi-tasking products! For example, buy a moisturizer with sunscreen; you'll avoid having to purchase two separate items, and you'll also save time in the morning. Tinted moisturizers eliminate the expense of foundation—find one with an SPF, and you've hit the jackpot! Other double duty favorites include shampoo and conditioner combos, tinted lip balms, hair and body washes, and rouge for cheeks and lips. Combine with workhorses like baking soda, olive oil and petroleum jelly, and cover all your beauty needs on a shoestring budget!

217 Do yoga

Forget the facelifts, Botox and anti-aging potions: relax away wrinkles with the power of yoga! The deep breathing exercises release tension from your face, melting away clenched jaws and furrowed brows. They also reduce stress and anxiety, lower blood pressure and relieve pain. If you can't get to a class, try some meditation at home. Sit in a comfortable position, with your back straight and gaze forward. Breathe slowly and deeply, clear your mind, and relax each part of your body, from your head down to your feet. Do this for ten minutes each day, and you'll look (and feel) ten years younger!

218 Drink plenty of water

Stay healthy and beautiful by drinking eight to ten glasses of water each day. Water makes up the majority of our bodies, and is essential to a variety of functions like digestion, absorption and circulation. It carries nutrients to our cells, and flushes impurities and toxins from our systems. Drinking water helps maintain muscle tone, lubricate joints, and lessen the chance of kidney stones. It also hydrates skin, maintaining its elasticity and giving it a natural, healthy glow. Best of all, this fabulous frugillionaire beauty regimen is virtually free!

219 Get your beauty sleep

They don't call it beauty sleep for nothing! Getting plenty of rest each night is one of the most effective ways to improve your overall health and appearance. You'll avoid bloodshot eyes and dark circles, and your skin will look smoother and more radiant. Proper rest also increases your energy, alertness and concentration. To get the recommended eight hours of sleep each night, avoid large meals, alcohol and caffeinated drinks before bedtime; eliminate light and noise from your bedroom; exercise daily; and maintain a regular sleep schedule. Go to bed early, and wake up gorgeous!

Chapter 7

ENTERTAINMENT (I)

Enjoying Arts and Culture on the Cheap

---

220 Go to music school concerts

Don't let your passion for Bach blow your budget; go to music school, as a spectator! Students training for music careers need live performance practice, so schools often hold free concerts to attract an audience for them. Tickets for shows at the prestigious Juilliard School, for example, are usually available at no charge. It's a great opportunity to enjoy an evening of opera, orchestra, choral or chamber music by up-and-coming stars—before they hit the professional circuit. Stick to well-respected or college-affiliated institutions for top-notch talent; or take the kids to a local children's recital for a fun night out!

221 Enjoy music al fresco

There's nothing more lovely than a symphony under the stars…especially when you don't have to pay for it! Summer is the season of free outdoor concerts: music-loving frugillionaires have their choice of classical, jazz, rock, reggae, country, swing, folk, blues and more. Groups giving al fresco performances range from small community ensembles, to the professional orchestras of major cities. The New York Philharmonic, Philadelphia Orchestra, and Boston Pops, for example, traditionally stage free summer shows on a grand scale. Check local papers and cultural websites to find events in your area.

222 Get rush tickets

Love the theater, but hate the high prices? For a Broadway experience on a budget, get last minute tickets! Box offices often release a limited number of deeply discounted tickets an hour or two before a performance. They're only available for select shows, so check with the venue for details. Obtaining such "rush" tickets, as they're called, requires some patience and flexibility: you'll usually need to wait in line, and you won't be able to choose your seats. But you'll be rewarded with the chance to see your favorite play, musical, opera or ballet—for a fraction of the price!

223 Buy a season subscription

What could be more fabulous than saving money, while supporting the arts? If you're an aficionado of the orchestra, opera or ballet, consider purchasing a subscription to the entire season; it's much cheaper than buying individual tickets for each show. Savings can range from 20 to 50 percent—and may add up to a free performance or two! As a bonus, subscribers are usually offered the best choice of seats, first access to popular shows, and the ability to exchange tickets if a scheduling conflict arises. Check your local tourism office or cultural alliance for special deals and discounts on subscription packages.

224 Be an usher

Get your cultural fix for free by becoming an usher! Many theaters, orchestras and dance troupes operate on tight budgets, and rely on volunteers to help with pre- and post-performance duties. If you're willing to pass out playbills and help ticket holders find their seats, you'll receive free admission to the show. It's also a wonderful way to meet people with similar interests, and support your local arts community. Call your favorite theater or cultural center to inquire about volunteer opportunities. Just think: you could enjoy an entire season of performances without spending a cent!

225 Support community theater

Support the arts in your hometown by attending local theater productions. Their inexpensive ticket prices let you enjoy the thrill of a live performance without breaking the bank. Furthermore, in small venues every seat is a good one; it sure beats having an obstructed view at the back of a Broadway theater! Stay after the show and mingle with the actors; you may even be able to take a backstage tour. Although not professional, the talent is usually good and the fun factor high—especially considering that Cleopatra may have cut your hair, or Macbeth delivered your mail, earlier that afternoon!

226 Attend community events

Hit the social circuit by attending free events in your hometown! Many communities sponsor weekly movie nights throughout the summer, showing free films in an outdoor setting. Others stage concerts and plays, or host craft fairs and arts festivals. Workshops, lectures, readings and discussion groups—for both kids and adults—are also popular offerings. Find out what's happening in your town on its website, in the local paper, and on community bulletin boards in libraries and government offices. Spice it up a little by "crashing" the events of neighboring towns; don't worry, all are welcome!

227 Use the university

Take advantage of the art, cultural and educational activities offered by local colleges and universities. Many learning institutions provide free access to their libraries, museums and galleries; others sponsor lectures, workshops and poetry readings. Some even offer adult-learning and continuing education programs for a nominal fee. Student art exhibits, and musical and theater performances, are a great alternative to pricey professional shows. You'll enjoy some wonderful entertainment, and catch an early glimpse of some rising stars. What's more, the campus experience will remind you of your own student days—when money was never essential to having fun!

228 Be an early bird

First-run flicks can be hard on your finances; save money by seeing the matinee. "Dinner and a movie" may be the norm, but film-loving frugillionaires reverse the order: catch the movie first, and then go out to eat. Afternoon shows are generally less expensive than evening ones—and less crowded as well! Cultural institutions also reward the early bird: music, theater and dance companies give discounted matinee performances, and some museums offer reduced (or free) admission on certain mornings. Inquire about these special rates, and get your entertainment "off-peak" for maximum savings!

229 Buy tickets in bulk

If you're a film buff—or have a large, movie-going family—
save big bucks by buying tickets in bulk. Some theaters offer
generous discounts for volumes of fifty tickets or more.
Arrange a joint purchase with friends or neighbors if you
won't use that many yourself; or suggest the idea to your
church, company or children's school. Just be sure to check
expiration dates and any restrictions: you may have to wait a
week to see new releases. You can also buy discounted
movie vouchers (usually in packs of five or ten) through
wholesale clubs, and organizations like the American
Automobile Association (AAA).

230 Know your discounts

Whether you're seeing a movie, going to a museum, or
spending the day at the zoo, be aware of any available
discounts! Most places offer reduced admission to senior
citizens, students and children, so take advantage of it if you
(or anyone in your party) qualifies. Veterans, military
personnel and their families, and members of clubs like the
American Automobile Association (AAA) are also commonly
eligible for lower rates. Be prepared to show appropriate
identification at the box office or entrance gate. Discounted
tickets may even be available through your place of
employment—ask your human resources department for
details.

231 Volunteer in a museum

If you're a museum buff on a minimum budget, consider volunteering! Donate a few hours of time each week to your favorite institution. Duties range from greeting visitors and taking tickets, to assisting with clerical and curatorial tasks. You may even become a museum guide, conducting tours of the permanent collection and special exhibitions. While you won't receive monetary compensation, you'll likely enjoy free admission, and have the unique opportunity to learn what goes on behind the scenes. Look into similar opportunities at zoos, parks, aquariums, history centers and botanical gardens—or anywhere else that suits your interests!

232 Become a member

If you attend a certain museum regularly, consider buying a membership; it usually includes free admission, and pays for itself in no time. Estimate how often you'll go, and do the math to compare your cost per visit to the regular entrance fee. Also consider other membership perks, such as reduced-price tickets to special exhibits; invitations to workshops, openings and exclusive events; and discounts in the museum shop and café. You may even be able to bring guests with you at no extra charge. It's a great way to enjoy those Van Goghs in VIP style—on a frugillionaire budget!

233 Eavesdrop on a tour

When you're in a museum, and a tour group enters the gallery—linger a while! The voice of a tour guide carries well through quiet spaces; you can't help but overhear their commentary on ancient Egyptian artifacts or Impressionist masterpieces. Idle near a neighboring display, and enjoy the free education. Alternatively, rent an audio tour; you'll receive headphones or a listening device with prerecorded information—at much less expense than a professional guide. If you have an iPod or mp3 player, even better: you can download free podcasts of tours for most major sites and museums.

234 Go when it's cheap

A little planning can save you a lot of money on entrance fees to museums, parks, zoos, gardens and more. Most cultural institutions offer free or discounted admission (or ask for a small donation in lieu of a ticket) on certain days. Contact individual museums for details, and plan your visits accordingly. Sign up on their websites to receive email newsletters and updates, which often include information on special deals. You'll also find coupons in local papers and mailers, especially during off-peak periods. Alternatively, attend with someone who has a membership—they can usually bring free guests!

235 Visit smaller museums

If you need a dose of culture—or just an interesting way to spend the afternoon—visit a small museum or history center. They're rarely crowded, and their entrance fees are a fraction of those of larger, more famous institutions. Such museums typically specialize in niche topics, like Alaskan art, Southern cuisine, silent films, early American textiles, railroad travel or minor league baseball. Some celebrate people and events of historical significance, such as Philadelphia's Betsy Ross House and the Texas Civil War Museum. Others—like the Giant Shoe Museum in Seattle—are just plain quirky!

236 View art in public buildings

You don't have to pay steep admission fees to enjoy great art. Some lovely collections are displayed in public buildings— free for the viewing! Federal buildings have a long history of housing important paintings and sculpture, while city halls and state offices often showcase the work of local artists. The lobbies of large companies are also worth a peek; some boast impressive collections in their corporate headquarters. And don't forget churches and cathedrals: these houses of worship are treasure troves of beautiful (and oftentimes famous) religious works of art.

237 View art outdoors

Avoid museum admission fees—by taking your love of art outdoors! Most major cities (and some smaller ones) have wonderful collections of public sculpture. These works range from statues of historical figures to more abstract, contemporary forms. Other displays are more ephemeral in nature: during a two-week period in 2005, for example, the famous artist Christo adorned New York's Central Park with 7500 saffron-colored gates. Consult the internet, or your local tourism office, for guides to open-air art in your area; and keep an eye on cultural listings for special outdoor installations and other temporary exhibits.

238 Go to church

For a rich cultural experience—at absolutely no cost—go to church! The architecture of cathedrals, synagogues and mosques is often quite spectacular, and the artwork inside can rival that of museums. You'll be able to enjoy ornate sculpture, gorgeous stained glass and magnificent paintings, without paying an admission fee. Go one step further and attend a service; it's a unique opportunity to experience the teachings and ceremonies of a faith different from your own. Church fairs celebrating the congregation's culture—like Polish, Russian or Orthodox Greek—can also be a lot of fun!

239 Go wine tasting

For a frugal date, or fun afternoon with friends, visit local vineyards—many offer free wine tasting to promote their products. You'll likely get quite an education from the vintner, as they're usually passionate about wine and love to chat with visitors. When a glass is poured for you, hold it up to the light and admire its color. Aerate the wine with a gentle swirl, then put your nose over the rim and breathe in its aroma. Finally, take a sip (not a gulp!) and savor its taste, sensation and finish. To enhance your experience, consult the internet (or books) beforehand for wine basics and tasting tips!

240 Go to book readings

For a frugal night out, attend a book or poetry reading at your local bookstore. Such events are held to help authors promote their latest work; admission is generally free, and there's no obligation to buy the book (unless, of course, you want to have it signed!). They often include a question-and-answer session, providing unique insight into the writer's inspiration and techniques. It's a wonderful opportunity to meet well-known authors, or discover those that are up-and-coming. Check your local bookstore's newsletter or calendar for a schedule of events.

241 Attend art openings

Enjoy a sophisticated night on the town—frugillionaire style—by attending art openings at local galleries. They're usually free to the public, and often serve complimentary wine and cheese. Best of all, the crowds and cocktail party atmosphere provide the freedom to browse, with no pressure to buy. For even more fun, participate in local "art walks." These events—during which *all* the galleries in a community open to the public—are typically held once a month. Spend the evening mingling with other enthusiasts, admiring the work of local artists, or just hanging out and feeling the vibe!

242 Attend CD release parties

If you love to see live bands—but are on a tight budget— attend CD release parties. They're promotional events, so there's usually no charge for admission; some even include complimentary refreshments. Don't worry if you've never heard of the band, or are unfamiliar with the genre; it's a great chance to expand your musical horizons! You may discover a new favorite, or catch some future stars before they hit the big time. Even if you don't become a fan, you'll enjoy the party atmosphere, and have a wonderful time mingling with fellow music lovers.

243 Find a festival

Festivals are a fabulous source of frugal entertainment! Celebrate the changing seasons with harvest festivals in fall, holiday festivals in winter, flower festivals in spring, and fruit festivals in summer. You can enjoy free or low-cost performances at music and theater festivals; admire the work of local artisans at craft fairs; and play connoisseur at wine, beer, cheese and chocolate tasting events. Attend ethnic festivals—like Irish, Italian, Chinese or African—to embrace your own culture, or learn about another. They feature traditional food, music and dancing, and are open to people of all backgrounds!

244 Visit the county fair

For a day's worth of entertainment, take the family to the county fair! It's cheaper than an amusement park, and offers a wide range of attractions: carnival rides, prize games, livestock shows, petting zoos, cook-offs, craft displays and more. Live concerts and other performances are often held in the evenings. Save money by purchasing tickets in advance, or attending during days (or hours) when admission is discounted. If possible, take public transit to avoid parking charges. Minimize food and drink costs by eating a large meal before you leave, packing snacks or picnic fare, and bringing your own bottle to refill at water fountains.

245 Enjoy a parade

Everyone loves a parade; they're flashy, they're fun, and—best of all—they're free! You'll find plenty on tap near any major holiday, like New Year's Day, St. Patrick's Day, the Fourth of July, Labor Day, Halloween, Thanksgiving and Christmas. Communities also organize them to honor firefighters, police officers, sports figures and military personnel; to commemorate the anniversaries of historic events; and to celebrate various cultures and ethnicities. The floats, drill teams, marching bands, pom-pom squads and cheering crowds ensure you and your family will have a fabulous time—without spending a dime!

246 See the fireworks

Fireworks displays are some of the best free entertainment around! The whole experience is a thrill: being outside after dark, the excitement of the crowd, the amazing pyrotechnics and the crashing booms that accompany them. Fortunately, communities embrace just about any chance to stage a show: New Year's Eve, Memorial Day, the Fourth of July, Labor Day, homecomings, sports events, festivals, concerts, grand openings and more. On the next occasion, take along a blanket and picnic basket, and make a fun (or romantic) night of it!

247 Cheer on local sports teams

Don't pay sky-high ticket prices, to support the sky-high salaries of professional sports teams! Attend a local sporting event instead: a high school football game, for example, is free fun for the whole family. It offers the excitement of live sports, plus a community atmosphere that can't be found in a fifty thousand-seat stadium. For a higher caliber of play, check out the athletic programs of local colleges. Consider yourself particularly lucky if you have a minor league team in your area. These players are just one step away from the majors—but tickets to their games are a fraction the price of the pros!

248 Watch outdoor races

If you're a sports fan on a budget, attend outdoor events with free admission like marathons, boat races and bike tournaments. They cover large areas, and usually occur on public streets and waterways—so it's next to impossible to charge spectators a fee. Tickets may be required for grandstand areas, but you can enjoy the event just as well (free of charge) anywhere else along the route. Choices range from charity runs, to professional events featuring top-notch athletes. Don't hesitate to try something new: a cycling, sculling or dragon boat race is an interesting and economical alternative to a day at the ballpark.

249 Buy season passes

If you frequent certain recreational facilities, buy season passes—they can yield significant savings over single tickets. To make sure you're getting a good deal: divide the total cost by the number of times you expect to visit, and compare to the regular admission price. Season passes are typically available for ice rinks, skating rinks, bowling alleys, miniature golf courses, zoos, ski resorts, swimming pools and amusement parks. In addition to unlimited access, pass holders often enjoy other benefits such as discounts on food, merchandise and guest tickets. If you're vacationing at a theme park like Disney World, purchase a multi-day pass; it's usually much cheaper than paying the daily rate!

250 Window shop

For the well-disciplined frugillionaire, window shopping can be a lovely, low-cost way to spend the afternoon. The allure of shopping lies mainly in the thrill of the hunt; in fact, the excitement often dissipates quickly after a purchase is made. So skip the buying part—you'll have just as much fun, and come home with a fuller wallet! Think of it like a museum trip: an opportunity to admire the beauty and design of well-crafted objects, without the possibility (or pressure) of ownership. It doesn't cost anything to look; just leave your cash and credit cards at home to avoid any temptation!

251 Browse flea markets

A flea market or antique show can provide hours of free entertainment—as long as you don't bring your wallet! Such events feature a diverse array of interesting vintage goods. You can while away the time admiring the craftsmanship of antique chairs or the hues of Tiffany lamps; browsing through old magazines, photos and postcards; or reminiscing over the toys and lunchboxes of your childhood. Vendors are usually happy to show off their treasures, and chat about their subjects of expertise. Since you're not there to spend money, you can simply relax and enjoy the experience!

252 Have fun on the farm

Live the rural life for a day—on a local farm! Many open their fields and orchards to the public, letting visitors harvest their own apples, strawberries, blueberries, pumpkins, and other fruits and vegetables. The experience is vastly more entertaining than going to the grocery store, and a great way to teach children that food doesn't grow on supermarket shelves. You'll not only have a ball playing farmer, you'll enjoy the delicious fruits of your labor: freshly-picked produce is much tastier, and healthier, than food that's shipped around the globe.

253 Visit a factory

Take a behind-the-scenes factory tour—it's a fascinating way to spend an afternoon! Many companies offer walkthroughs of their plants, and demonstrations of their manufacturing techniques, to visitors. You can watch experts build pianos, distill whiskey, print newspapers, blow glass, churn ice cream, or brew beer; or see first-hand how crayons, guitars, motorcycles, toothpaste or jelly beans are made. Best of all, most tours are family-friendly and free of charge—some even include complimentary samples at the end! To find options in your area, simply search the internet or contact your local tourism office.

254 People watch

Looking for some low-key, no-cost entertainment? Sit on a bench and watch the world go by! People watching is a fascinating way to pass the time, and a park, public square or city street affords plenty of activity on which to focus your attention. If you're interested in fashion, observe the outfits of passersby; the unique stylings of everyday people are infinitely more interesting than a runway show. Or exercise your creativity, and dream up stories for those you behold— imagine who they are, what they do, and where they're going. Trade tales with a partner for double the fun!

255 Ride the subway

For a frugal adventure, ride your local train or subway to an unfamiliar station. Your transit experience is likely limited to one or two stops; why not see what interesting sights the others hold? Pick places at random, or venture out to the termination points of each line. (Do some research beforehand for safety's sake; it's not much fun to set foot in a crime-ridden area!) Stations are often located in bustling towns and business districts, providing a wonderful opportunity to browse the shops, visit a café, and soak up the atmosphere of the local main street!

256 Go bird-watching

For some frugal fun, try bird-watching! Obtain a field guide from the library, and borrow a pair of binoculars from friends or family; if you can't manage the latter, your own two eyes will do just fine. Before venturing out, learn about the different species, and know where to find them in your book; you won't have time to flip through hundreds of pages before that Golden-winged Warbler flies away! When you're ready, head out to your chosen location—park, forest or your own backyard—and simply watch and listen. Try to identify the birds you see, using clues like shape, size, plumage, behavior and call. It's challenging at first, but gets easier and more rewarding as you gain experience!

257 Go letterboxing

Letterboxing is an enjoyable outdoor activity that offers the thrill of a treasure hunt, at little to no cost. Participants hide waterproof boxes—containing a logbook, rubber stamp and optional goodies—in remote places, and publish clues to their locations on the internet. Hunters decipher the clues and search for the boxes; a map and compass, or hike in the woods, are sometimes involved. Upon uncovering a box, the finder records his discovery by stamping a logbook, or in some cases, making an entry on the appropriate letterboxing website. It's great entertainment for both children and adults!

258 Walk for charity

Participate in a charity walk—it's a fabulous way to spend the day, while raising money for a good cause! Events support a range of philanthropic aims, from disease awareness and medical research to social issues and human rights. Some request a small donation or registration fee, while others ask you to sign up corporate or individual sponsors. If you're athletically inclined, consider a more challenging run, marathon or bike ride. You'll not only help the charity of your choice; you'll stay in shape, and achieve personal fitness goals, without the expense of a gym membership!

259 Volunteer

Donate your time to a worthy cause—you'll be much richer for the experience! Volunteer possibilities abound: you can serve meals at a soup kitchen, walk dogs at an animal shelter, build houses for low-income families, teach computer skills to seniors, provide companionship to the housebound, mentor inner-city youth…the list goes on and on! To find out how you can help, contact national nonprofits or community organizations. Alternatively, use an online service like VolunteerMatch.org: input your location and interests, and you'll receive information on opportunities in your area.

Chapter 8

ENTERTAINMENT (II)

Having a Blast
without Breaking the Bank

260 Throw a non-dinner party

Entertain on a shoestring by throwing a non-dinner party! Host your gathering during mid-afternoon, cocktail, or late-night hours to avoid the expense of providing a meal. If you limit fare to snacks and hors d'oeuvres, or coffee and dessert, you'll slash your refreshment budget. This frugillionaire strategy is particularly effective for weddings and other large events. By purchasing pre-prepared food, and serving it buffet style, you'll eliminate the need for full catering services. Plan the menu so that minimal plates and utensils suffice, and you'll also cut the costs of renting tableware.

261 Be your own DJ

If you're hosting a party, save big bucks by skipping the live band or disc jockey! Instead, connect your iPod or mp3 player to your speaker system, and be your own DJ. Search your collection for music appropriate to the mood and occasion; for more variety, purchase additional songs online. At around $1 per song, you can build a party-worthy playlist that's well within your budget. If the venue is large (like a banquet hall), you may need to rent a more powerful sound system; however, it will still be much cheaper than hiring professional entertainment!

262 Host a movie night

Recreate the excitement of going to the movies—in your own home! Hosting a movie night is frugal, fabulous, and loads of fun. Rent a DVD, and invite an audience of family, friends and neighbors. Make plenty of popcorn (the aroma is part of the experience!), and encourage attendees to "sneak in" the candy and beverages of their choice. Dim the lights and turn up the sound for maximum movie ambience. If you decide to make it a regular event, pick a theme for the upcoming week—like adventure, romance, comedy or western—and take film suggestions from participants.

263 Host a TV party

Invite friends over to watch popular events on television—it's a frugal alternative to hitting the town! The possibilities are endless, and include sports championships and all-star games, movie and music awards shows, pay-per-view events, political debates, and the premieres and finales of popular television series. Minimize refreshment expense by asking guests to bring snacks for the buffet table. For a little more fun, encourage attendees to don apparel, or bring props, appropriate to the theme: jerseys and pennants for sports nights, glitz and glamour for the Oscars, or political paraphernalia for debates and election returns.

264 Play games

Looking for a low-cost way to entertain guests, or keep children occupied? Bring out a deck of cards, or an old-fashioned board game. An afternoon of bridge, poker, rummy or go fish doesn't cost a dime; use chips, instead of money, where wagering is involved. If you've forgotten how to play, consult the internet for instructions and rules. A Scrabble or Monopoly board can also provide hours of enjoyment; dig it out, dust it off, and let the fun begin! Alternatively, try parlor games like Twenty Questions or charades—they have a wonderful retro appeal, and are suitable for all ages.

265 Dance!

Put on some music and dance! When it comes to entertainment, there's nothing more frugal—or fun—than cutting a rug with your favorite partner. It lifts your spirits, burns calories, and reminds you how wonderful it is to be alive. Have a blast learning traditional dances like the waltz, cha-cha or tango; for step-by-step instructions, consult the internet, or borrow a book or DVD from the library. If your local college or community center offers low-cost dance classes, sign up. It's a great way to stay fit, meet interesting people, and master some new moves!

266 Enjoy being at home

Consider how much you spend on your house, including mortgage or rent, property taxes, utilities, maintenance, furnishings and décor. It's likely a sizable chunk of your earnings—so you may as well squeeze some entertainment value from it! Instead of going out for dinner, a movie or other costly activity, enjoy some recreation time at home. Sit on the porch and read a book, have a relaxing soak in your tub, or curl up on the couch and watch a DVD. Play games with your kids, make a home-cooked meal, or just lounge in the backyard and listen to the birds. Your home is your castle, so have some fun "staying in!"

267 Have a "no-spend" weekend

Challenge yourself and your family to a "no spend" weekend, and you'll realize that having fun doesn't require money! Hang out in the backyard or a local park; bring a picnic lunch if you spend the day out. Read books, play games, or watch DVDs you already own. Take a long walk, a long bath, or a long nap. Make each meal an event: take pleasure in the entire process, from preparing the ingredients to savoring the results. Chances are, you'll be just as happy—and certainly richer—than if you'd spent the weekend in restaurants, movies or the mall!

268 Be a good neighbor

Instead of going shopping on weekends, hang around your neighborhood! Chat with the family down the street, or invite over the couple that just moved in. Assist the elderly woman next door with a difficult household task. It's a frugal, and fulfilling, way to pass the time. What's more, your efforts will pay dividends: good neighbors are helping hands when you're in need, and watchful eyes when you're away. If you're having trouble meeting people, organize a block party. Get permission from your town, pass out flyers announcing the event, and plan an afternoon of neighborly fun!

269 Love your library

Fall in love with your library! Take advantage of the amazing variety of books, magazines, CDs and DVDs—all free for the borrowing! If you don't see the title you're looking for, just ask: most libraries are part of county networks and will transfer books between branches. Fill out an Interlibrary Loan Request to obtain materials from outside the county system. Many libraries now have their catalogs online, so you can browse from the comfort of your own home. When you find a book you'd like to borrow, just click to request it—it'll be held at your local branch for pick-up. How's that for convenience?

270 Love your library more

The library isn't just for borrowing; it can also provide hours of free entertainment! Spend an afternoon browsing the collection; some institutions have incredible amounts of reference and research materials. Many also stage exhibits of art, rare books or historical documents. If you just want to relax, grab a stack of magazines and a comfy chair, or surf the internet. Visit libraries in neighboring towns for variety; you may not be able to borrow from them, but you can certainly enjoy their resources for the day. With all they have to offer, libraries are truly a frugillionaire's playground!

271 Say no to newspapers

Save your money—and some trees—by canceling your newspaper subscription! Most publications put the same content on their websites, so why pay for something you can get for free? You can even sign up to receive headlines by email, or breaking news on your mobile phone. Plus, on the internet you're not limited to your local daily; thousands of papers are available, from all over the world! Sample the international press for a different (and often enlightening) perspective on domestic and world events. If you're reluctant to ditch the printed page entirely, start by paring down to a Sunday- or weekend-only subscription.

272 Minimize magazines

Magazines keep us up-to-date on the topics that interest us—be they business, science, politics, fashion, sports or home design. How can you save cash, while staying current on your favorite subjects? Skip the subscriptions, and visit the websites of your favorite periodicals instead—in most cases, you'll be able to read the same articles for free. Alternatively, drop by your local library; you can peruse current issues in the reading room, or borrow back copies for home. If family and friends have subscriptions, ask for the magazines they've finished reading; they'll usually be happy to pass them along!

273 Swap books, CDs and DVDs with friends

Diversify your book, music or video library—by swapping with friends and family! The next time you spy an interesting tome on your sister's bookshelf, ask to borrow it instead of purchasing your own copy. Offer something from your own collection in return. Or arrange a trading system with one or more friends, and regularly pass along finished books to each other. A media party can also be fun: have everyone bring a selection of CDs or DVDs to share with the group. Each guest picks a few to take home, then returns them at the next get-together. It's a wonderful way to stretch your entertainment dollars!

274 Swap books, CDs and DVDs online

Expand your options further by swapping books, CDs and DVDs online! Numerous websites offer trading services; enter "swap books online" or "swap DVDs online" in your favorite search engine for a comprehensive list. For best results, sign up with a popular site like Swaptree.com or paperbackswap.com—the larger the membership, the greater the trade possibilities. List the items you're willing to give, and those you'd like to receive; some sites arrange a direct swap, while others use a credit system. The service is free of charge, so your only expense is shipping; use USPS Media Mail for the cheapest rates.

275 Rent DVDs from kiosks

Rent movies for $1 a night from self-service kiosks like Redbox—they dispense DVDs like a vending machine. Simply follow the instructions on the touch screen to make your selection, swipe your credit card, and retrieve your movie. After you've enjoyed it, just return it to any of the company's kiosks. Some services even let you browse their selection online, and reserve your copy in advance. These efficient, economical movie machines can be found in supermarkets, convenience stores, pharmacies and fast food restaurants. Rent and return DVDs while running other errands, and you won't even use extra gas!

276 Rent DVDs online

If you watch a lot of movies, an online subscription service may be less expensive than your local video store. Companies like Netflix.com offer DVD rentals for a monthly fee. Select movies on their website, and receive them in the mail; prepaid envelopes are supplied for sending them back. Some titles are even available for immediate viewing on your personal computer. This "digital delivery" option eliminates the physical DVD—and the hassle of picking it up, dropping it off, or mailing it back—entirely! Subscription rates vary by rental volume; do the math, and choose the most economical plan for your needs.

277 Surf the internet

If you're already paying for internet access—or can obtain it free of charge at a library or wireless hotspot—take advantage of its recreational value! You'll find plenty of websites that let you play games, watch videos, or listen to music to your heart's content. Newspapers, magazines—even entire books—are available online for your reading pleasure. You can also participate in discussion forums on your favorite subjects, and chat with fellow enthusiasts on almost any conceivable topic. And if you enjoy perusing the opinions, experiences, and random thoughts of others, there's no shortage of blogs to keep you entertained!

278 Listen to podcasts

Explore the wonderful world of podcasts—they offer unlimited hours of free entertainment! Podcasts are digital audio files that can be downloaded from the internet, and listened to on your computer or mp3 player. Hundreds of thousands are available, on a wide range of topics: news, sports, politics, technology, arts, culture, language, music, science, religion, travel, food and more. Anyone with a microphone can publish a podcast—from individuals to major media outlets—so the variety is enormous. Subscribe to a series, and new shows will be automatically downloaded to your computer as they become available.

279 Download free lectures

How would you like to attend poetry or philosophy classes, or seminars taught by the brightest thinkers of our time, at absolutely no cost? You can, by downloading college lectures from the internet! Premier universities like Yale, Harvard, MIT and Stanford offer academic materials, video lectures—and in some cases, entire courses—online. They're free of charge, and accessible to anyone with an internet connection. You won't receive credits or a degree, but you'll enjoy a fabulous learning experience—without the stress of taking notes, cramming for exams, or paying tuition!

280 Start a blog

Start a blog, and share your interests, expertise and opinions with the world! A blog (short for "Web log") is a personal website on which you write regular entries about a particular topic. You can provide commentary on current events, chronicle your weight loss efforts, or wax poetic on the joys of raising kids—the possibilities are endless! Companies like Blogger.com and Wordpress.com offer free websites and software, enabling you to get up and running in minutes. What's more: you can even host ads on your blog, and earn a little extra income toward your frugillionaire goals!

281 Write in a journal

Looking for an inexpensive hobby? Sit down with paper, pen and your own thoughts. Journal writing is the adult version of that diary you kept in the sixth grade. To get started, just write down whatever's on your mind—whether it's existential musings on the meaning of life, or what you had for breakfast. Describe the weather, your day's activities, or your current mood, and feel free to go off on tangents as they arise. Write as regularly as possible—it lowers stress, and can help you identify and work through difficult emotions. It may even save you on therapy bills down the road!

282 Write a letter

Write someone a letter! In this age of email and text messaging, it's a real novelty to send a piece of old-fashioned correspondence. Before you begin, take a few minutes to plan what you'll say—it's harder to "delete" a handwritten line than a typed one. Tell the recipient about recent events in your life, reminisce about old times, or just let them know you're thinking about them. If you prefer, write letters you don't intend to mail—to people who are living or deceased, familiar or famous, real or fictional. For example, pen your thoughts on politics to Abraham Lincoln, or ask the Buddha for career advice!

283 Write a poem

Entertain yourself, and express your creativity, by writing poetry! Start by choosing a theme, be it an ode to spring flowers, a confession of love, or a personal revelation. Write down words and phrases describing your subject; then arrange them in traditional poetic form, such as sonnet, limerick or haiku. Use techniques like rhyme, meter and alliteration, or simply write in free verse. If you'd like some feedback—but are too shy to share with friends or family—join an online poetry group. You can post your work (signed or anonymous), and receive advice and opinions from fellow bards!

284 Sketch, doodle or draw

For hours of free fun, grab a pencil and paper and start sketching! Look around your house or garden for inspiration—fruit, flowers and people make good subjects. You can also draw from photos or memory. If you're light on technique, borrow an introductory book from the library, or search the internet for tutorials. Once you've learned the basics of shading, perspective and form, you'll be able to tackle three-dimensional objects with confidence. If nothing else, try some swirls, curls and freeform patterns; doodling can be very relaxing, and doesn't cost a dime!

285 Read a good book

Curl up with a good book! Re-read those classic works of literature you studied in high school; you'll find you have a greater appreciation and understanding of them as an adult. If you prefer nonfiction, pick up some tomes on history, travel, philosophy, or whatever suits your interests. Save money by borrowing from the library, swapping with friends, or buying secondhand; websites like Amazon.com and Half.com offer plenty of used copies. A crease on the cover or note in the margin doesn't make it any less readable! When you're finished with the book, resell it online to recoup your costs.

286 Get crafty

Make something by hand—it's fun, frugal, and a great creative outlet! Choose a craft that involves simple, inexpensive materials, so you don't spend a fortune on supplies. Tackle the art of origami, for example, with extra scraps of paper; practice calligraphy with a sketchpad and pen; or knit a beautiful scarf from a single ball of yarn. Pillows can be sewn from leftover fabric, and potpourri made with dried flowers and herbs. Borrow books from the library, or search the internet, for ideas and instructions. Crafting is not only a relaxing hobby—the fruits of your labor make wonderful gifts!

287 Tackle a puzzle

Pass the time with a challenging puzzle; you'll give your mind a workout, and your wallet a rest! Thousands of crossword and sudoku puzzles are available free of charge on the internet. Print them out, or complete them online; some sites even time how quickly you can finish them. Jigsaw puzzles are another absorbing activity. Obtain them secondhand from garage sales and thrift stores, or complete them in cyberspace: move the pieces with your mouse, and fit them together, right on your computer screen! Try anagrams, doublets, cryptograms, riddles and other brainteasers for more frugal fun.

288 Play photographer

Grab your digital camera, and play photographer for a day! Looking through the lens transforms your perception: you'll see new beauty in your surroundings, and notice colors, patterns and details that previously escaped your attention. Walk around your neighborhood, and choose interesting foliage, architecture or other subjects to shoot. Take as many pictures as you like; with digital technology, there's no need to worry about processing costs. Use websites like Flickr.com and Shutterfly.com to share your snapshots with friends—or the world—free of charge!

289 Learn a foreign language

Instead of shopping in your leisure time, learn a new language. It's easier on the budget, and better exercise for your mind, than deciding which shoes to buy! The library is an excellent source of introductory books and CDs, and you'll find countless tutorials, podcasts and practice drills on the internet. Whether you're tackling French, Italian, Russian or Swahili, look for a community group to practice your conversation skills. You can also join online discussion forums to chat, and conjugate verbs, with fellow students. Just imagine how you'll dazzle your friends by ordering sushi in flawless Japanese!

290 Learn a new skill

Spend your spare time like a frugillionaire, and learn a new skill! If you'd love to be able to knit, pick up some needles and practice your stitches. If you dream of traveling to Paris, devote some hours to studying French. Books on languages, crafts and other hobbies are readily available at your local library, and you'll find internet tutorials on a plethora of pursuits: baking bread, doing yoga, making soap, playing chess, growing orchids, taking photos, writing music and more! If you learn better in a group, check out your local college or community center for free or low-cost classes.

291 Join a discussion group

Join a local discussion group—it's a frugal way to explore your interests and meet new friends! Such groups organize around a particular topic, such as books, health, investing, crafting, films, weight loss, religion, frugality, politics, parenting or career development. They usually convene on a regular basis, providing you with the opportunity to exchange information, obtain support, or pursue your hobby with like-minded individuals. Some even organize outings and field trips related to the subject of interest. Find groups in your area by searching websites like Meetup.com, or browsing community bulletin boards and calendars.

292 Learn a musical instrument

Learning to play a musical instrument can be a very frugal endeavor! There's no need for top-of-the-line equipment when you're just starting out; used guitars, violins, cellos and more can be had on the cheap. Search Craigslist.com and Freecycle.com, and you'll find some fabulous bargains and freebies. In fact, people are often happy to give away old instruments to enthusiastic students! Check out community centers for low-cost lessons, or go online—video tutorials for popular instruments are plentiful. Once you've learned the basics, join an informal music group for further practice and pointers.

293 Join a music group

Dust off that violin, or warm up those vocal chords, and join a local music group! You don't need a degree from Juilliard—or anywhere else, for that matter—to participate in your community's orchestra. Musicians of all levels are generally welcome, and auditions rarely required. Church and local choirs are great options for those who can carry a tune. If you're shy about performing before an audience, get some practice first in an informal setting: find a group that meets regularly to play popular tunes and folk songs for their own enjoyment. Simply show up with your instrument and join the fun!

294 Join a sports league

Spend your Saturdays shooting hoops or playing softball, instead of spending money! Recreational sports leagues focus on fun, rather than competition, and provide a great opportunity to socialize and stay fit. Check local gyms and community centers, or search online, to find teams in your area. Alternatively, look for "pick up" games, where anyone can show up and play; they're ideal for those who can't make a full-season commitment. Ask around your workplace as well: many companies participate in sports leagues, or organize athletic activities for employees.

295 Enjoy the great outdoors

For some fabulous, frugal recreation, go outside! Head to the park and toss around a Frisbee, or spend an afternoon cooking out and relaxing in your own backyard. You can also hike, bike, skate, fish or camp at little to no cost. Or simply pass the time with a leisurely stroll around your city or neighborhood—it's more interesting (and certainly cheaper) than going to the movies or the mall. Observe the details of houses, gardens and public spaces; notice which trees, plants and flowers are in bloom; or strike up a conversation with those you meet along the way!

296 Take a nature walk

Take a nature walk—it's a rewarding experience for your mind, body and soul! Visit a public park, wilderness trail, arboretum or garden, and open your senses to all nature has to offer. Study the bark on the trees, the leaves on the plants, and the blooms on the flowers. Listen to the call of the birds, the crackle of leaves underfoot, and the sounds of scurrying wildlife. Breathe in the fresh air, and savor the scent of blossoms, foliage and soil. You'll enjoy a lovely afternoon, get some wonderful exercise, and gain a renewed appreciation for life—all without spending a dime!

297 Ride your bike

You likely spent many happy hours as a kid riding your bike around your neighborhood. Well, get out the two-wheeler, and recapture that childhood joy! There's no need to set any speed or distance records; simply meander through the streets and enjoy the scenery. Or, attach a basket or panniers to your bike and run some errands—it's cheaper, and more pleasurable, than driving. If you don't currently own a bike, you can find a bargain-priced one on Craigslist.com, through the classifieds, or at garage and yard sales. Local bike shops often carry a secondhand selection, and can also help outfit you with a helmet and other gear.

298 Go for a swim

Swimming is a great workout for the heart, lungs and muscles—not to mention a lot of fun! You don't need to join a country club to get into the water; many communities have pools available to residents at little or no cost. Taking a dip in a lake, or the ocean, is another frugal option. Alternatively, find a gym with a pool, and obtain a trial membership; you'll be able to use the facilities free of charge for a short period (usually a few days to a week). If all else fails, find a friend who belongs to a swim club, and tag along as a guest—just be sure to return the favor!

299 Play in the park

While away the hours playing in the park—it doesn't cost a thing, and fills your entire being with joy! Pretend you're five years old again, with no care in the world but to run around, laugh and have fun. Ride on the swings, roll in the grass, or frolic with your dog. Toss a Frisbee with friends, or play catch, tag or hide-and-seek. It's a wonderful way to forget your worries, and enjoy life like a frugillionaire. If you have kids, join them in their activities instead of watching from the sidelines; you'll have a blast, and make some priceless memories!

300 Stargaze

What could be more wonderful than an evening of stargazing? It not only makes for a romantic date; it can provide frugal fun for the whole family! Before venturing out, learn what to look for in your local night sky: borrow an astronomy book from the library, or consult the internet for constellation guides. There's no need to obtain a telescope, as plenty of stars, planets and galaxies are visible to the naked eye. For the best experience, choose a cloudless evening, and a location with as little ambient light as possible. If you time your outing during a meteor shower, you may even spot some shooting stars!

301 Romance your partner

Spend a special evening with your significant other! You don't have to go to a fancy restaurant to enjoy a romantic night; dim the lights, turn on some music, and set the mood at home. Dress up as if you're hitting the town, and flirt like it's your first date. Take pleasure in preparing a meal together; cooking as a couple can be a sensuous experience, and a powerful aphrodisiac. Dine slowly by candlelight, then top off the evening with some frugal—and fabulous—fun in the bedroom. A night of passion doesn't cost a penny, and it's a great investment in the health of your relationship!

Chapter 9

TRANSPORTATION

Saving Money
When You're on the Move

---

302 Take public transit

Be a frugillionaire with your own chauffeur—by taking public transit! Ride the bus, train or subway and let someone else do the driving. Instead of fighting rush hour traffic, you'll be able to sit back, relax and enjoy the scenery. Pass the time by catching up on a novel, chatting with a fellow passenger, or listening to some favorite tunes. Contact your local transportation authority—or look on their website—for information on schedules, stations and tickets. Not only will you save a fortune on gas and parking; you'll also gain some wonderful relaxation time!

303 Ask about public transit incentives

Many companies offer subsidies, or monetary compensation, for employees who take public transit to work. This benefit is typically tax-free, and is distributed in the form of passes, vouchers or cash. Alternatively, you may be able to deduct public transit costs from your paycheck in pre-tax dollars. Paying your commuting costs this way reduces the amount of your federal (and sometimes state and local) income tax. Ask your employer or local transit authority about available programs. You can also contact the American Public Transportation Association, or visit CommuterChoice.com, for more information.

304 Get a transit pass

If you're a regular rider of mass transit, save money on tickets by purchasing a pass! Some passes cover a certain number of rides at a discounted rate. Others allow unlimited trips over a weekly or monthly time period. Passes in the form of reloadable "smart cards" let you purchase additional rides with a debit or credit card. Some even have an Autoload feature, which automatically tops up the card when the balance falls below a certain threshold. Find out what kind of discount passes your local transit authority offers; then do the math to choose what's best for you!

305 Carpool to work

Carpool to work with colleagues who live in your area. If you're going to sit in rush hour traffic, you may as well have company! Take turns being chauffeur, or share gas and maintenance costs with the primary driver. Establish a time schedule, and make sure all participants have each other's cell phone numbers. You'll need to be able to contact each other promptly if someone calls in sick or takes the day off. If necessary, look outside your company for fellow carpoolers: websites like eRideShare.com and Carpoolconnect.com match riders based on work schedules and locations.

306 Join a car share

If you use your car infrequently, get rid of it altogether and join a car share program. Popular in urban areas, car shares—like Zipcar—let members rent cars by the day or hour. The cars are distributed throughout metro areas in designated parking spaces. Simply go online to reserve one; then use the key or smart card (provided when you sign up) to unlock the doors and drive away. Gas and insurance are included in the rates. If you only need a car for occasional errands, it makes more sense to borrow than own—you'll save tons of money on registration, insurance, maintenance and parking costs!

307 Become a one-car household

Slash your family's expenses by becoming a one-car household! You'll eliminate the cost of purchasing, leasing and financing additional cars; and you'll also save on taxes, insurance, registration, repairs and maintenance. All it takes is a little planning: couples can arrange their schedules to ride to work together, or one can find an alternative method of transportation (like biking or public transit). Use a school bus service for kids, or arrange a carpool with other parents. If you can't get by with one car where you live now, make it a goal for the next time you move—and choose a location that makes it possible!

308 Commute off-peak

Save money, time and frustration by commuting off-peak! Traveling when roads are less congested reduces wear and tear on your car, and increases your fuel efficiency. Public transit tickets are also usually less expensive during non-commuter hours. If it's okay with your employer, start your workday an hour or two earlier (or later) to avoid rush hour traffic. Or ask if you can work the first, or final, hours of each day from home. A four-day schedule is another option: working ten-hour shifts (instead of the usual 9-to-5) avoids peak traffic times, and eliminates an entire day of driving!

309 Telecommute

Telecommuting can mean big savings! If your employer allows it, work from home one or more days per week. You'll reduce your gas, parking, maintenance, insurance, and public transit costs; and you'll also save on snacks, coffee and lunches out. If you work from home often, you can even curtail your spending on professional clothing (and dry cleaning services)! To transmit data and stay in touch with the office, you'll need a computer, phone line and high-speed internet connection. See if your employer will cover some of these home office expenses; if not, you may be able to deduct them from your income taxes.

310 Commute by bike

Leave the car at home, and pedal to work instead! It's better for your wallet, the environment, and your health. You'll save substantial money on car- and commuter-related costs. In addition, you'll burn a ton of calories, build up your leg muscles and get a great cardiovascular workout—without the expense of joining a gym! Obtain a bike on the cheap through Craigslist.com, Freecycle.com, thrift stores and garage sales; or ask friends and family if you can borrow one they're not using. Remember to wear a helmet and practice safe biking techniques, and you'll arrive at your destination fit, flush and fabulous!

311 Walk

Don't take your car on shorter errands—take a stroll instead! Walking is terrific exercise: it helps you lose weight, control blood pressure, and reduce the risk of heart attack, stroke and disease. It also lowers stress, strengthens bones and tones muscles. You'll not only save money on gas or public transit; you'll reduce future health care costs, and your legs will look fantastic! Walking to the store also keeps your spending in check, since you can't buy more than you can physically carry home. Feel particularly fortunate if you're a city dweller, since you can accomplish just about anything on foot!

312 Get a scooter

Be très chic, and trade in that gas-guzzler for a scooter! Look to stylish residents of Paris, Rome and other European cities for inspiration; they've used scooters for years to beat high gas prices. They're perfect for short commutes and local errands, and pay for themselves quickly in fuel savings. It takes only a few dollars to fill the tank, and most models get about 75-100 miles per gallon. Best of all, they're fun to drive, and easy to maneuver and park. So hop on your Vespa, and motor around to your heart's content— being a frugillionaire can be very fashionable!

313 Consolidate errands

How often do you visit the dry cleaners in the morning; run out later for milk; then make an evening drive to the video store? With a little planning, you can save money on gas by consolidating errands into one trip. Simply keep a to-do list with you in the car; that way, you can take care of everything at once while you're out on the road. And to reduce those "emergency runs" to the grocery store, plan your meals and make a list before you go shopping. For maximum savings: run errands during your daily commute, and schedule your stops in the most efficient order.

314 Drive a smaller car

When it comes to cars, think small for big savings! Ditch the sport utility vehicle, and downsize to a compact. Small cars are lighter and more fuel-efficient than their larger counterparts—letting you drive many more miles on each gallon of gas. They're also easier to handle, and less expensive to purchase and maintain. Advancements in design and technology have increased the comfort, performance and safety of compact vehicles. Just be sure to check out crash test ratings for the model you're considering, and invest in features like stability control and side-impact airbags.

315 Lose the lead foot

Drive slower to save money on gas! Resist the urge to put pedal to the metal—fuel economy drops significantly at higher speeds. Wind resistance increases exponentially over 55 mph, making the engine work harder to maintain the car's velocity. Therefore, the faster you drive, the fewer miles per gallon you'll get—and the more gas you'll use to reach your destination. For maximum safety and savings, stay in the right lane and stick to the speed limit. You'll lower your stress, your fuel costs, and your risk of getting a ticket!

316 Drive at a constant speed

Ditch bad driving habits—they're detrimental to your wallet and your safety! Quick acceleration and hard braking increase wear and tear on your car, and reduce fuel economy. Avoid aggressive moves, like speeding up to pass cars, then jamming on the brakes when traffic slows. And don't take off at one stoplight, only to screech to a halt at the next. Strive to be a smooth operator instead: accelerate and decelerate gradually, and maintain a constant speed whenever possible. Anticipate lights so you can coast to a stop, and use cruise control on highways to reduce fuel consumption.

317 Check your tire pressure

Keep your tires properly inflated; you'll improve your gas mileage, and save money at the pump! Check the pressure on a regular basis, ideally when tires are cold. All you need is a simple tire gauge, which can be purchased inexpensively at your local auto parts store. Remove the cap from your tire's valve, and press the gauge firmly onto the stem to stop the flow of air. Note the reading, and compare to the recommended PSI (usually written on the side of the tire). Add air if necessary, and replace the cap. This simple process saves gas, increases safety, and reduces wear-and-tear on your tires.

318 Change your air filter

Decrease your fuel costs by changing your air filter! A car's air filter keeps dirt, bugs and other impurities out of the engine—protecting it from damage, and allowing it to operate at peak efficiency. When the filter is clogged, the engine must work harder, and fuel efficiency is decreased. Maximize your gas mileage by checking your filter regularly and replacing it when dirty. Have a local mechanic perform the work at your next oil change, or consult your car's manual for do-it-yourself instructions. New air filters are inexpensive and readily available at auto parts stores.

319 Lighten your load

Give your car a minimalist makeover, for maximum fuel efficiency! If you have a trunk full of tools and sporting equipment, or a backseat strewn with toys, books and other sundries, it's time to clear out the clutter. Lugging around extra weight reduces your car's fuel economy. If you lighten the load, you'll improve your mileage and lower your gas costs. And don't forget about the roof rack: it not only weighs you down, it affects your car's aerodynamics. Remove it when it's not in use, instead of leaving it on year round.

320 Shop for gas online

You can't buy your gas online—but you can certainly shop around for the best deals! Check out websites like GasBuddy.com that monitor the cost of fueling up in your area. Simply type in your zip code, and obtain the locations of the least expensive stations. Search along the entire route of your commute, so you can plan ahead for the cheapest fill-up. That way, you won't need to cruise around—wasting time and money—looking for the best price. But remember: no matter how low a station's price, it's no bargain if it's miles out of your way!

321 Get a gas rebate credit card

Frugillionaires lessen the pain at the pump, by getting rewards when filling their tanks! Many credit cards offer rebate programs—like 1 to 5 percent cash back—on gasoline purchases. That can add up quickly when prices are high! Read the fine print to make sure the offer's a good deal; an annual fee or high interest rate can completely wipe out any savings. And by all means, pay your balance in full each month. It doesn't make sense to save a few dollars on gas, and then pay interest on it. Skip the credit cards altogether if your local station offers discounts for cash.

322 Maintain your car

Keep your car in tip-top shape—you'll extend its life and avoid costly repairs. Tune-ups, oil changes and other routine maintenance help prevent future breakdowns. Have fluids, belts, filters, batteries and brakes checked regularly; consult your owner's manual or a mechanic for recommended service schedules. It's much less expensive to find (and fix) small problems before they become big ones. Keep written records of all maintenance and repairs, as they'll aid in diagnosing any trouble that arises. Give your car a little TLC, and you'll be rewarded with years of reliable service!

323 Find an honest mechanic

Many of us have no idea what's going on under our hoods; we rely on auto shops to fix our cars and bill us fairly. Short of DIY, the best way to save money is to find an honest mechanic! Ask friends and family for recommendations; they'll be quick to sing the praises of competent, trustworthy individuals. Then build a relationship with your mechanic *before* your car breaks down, by taking it in for regular tune-ups and oil changes. Someone who performs routine maintenance on your car will be more familiar with it, and better able to diagnose future problems.

324 Wash your own car

Don't pay for a pricey car wash; it's more frugal—and fabulous—to do it yourself! Grab soap, sponge and a bucket of water, put on some music, and have a blast! While you're at it, wash your spouse's car too; little acts of kindness pay huge dividends. If you're an apartment dweller without access to a hose, find a self-service car wash in the area. For a small fee, you'll get soap, water and wax from an automated machine. Or keep an eye out for community- and charity-sponsored washes; they're cheaper than a professional cleaning, and your money will go to a good cause!

325 Shop smart for a new car

If you're in the market for a new car, a little research—and a little haggling—can save you big bucks! Before you hit the showroom, find out the vehicle's invoice price. In theory, this is what the dealer pays for the car; but with holdbacks and incentives, their cost is usually even less. Start your negotiations at the invoice (rather than sticker) price, and you can save thousands of dollars. If you prefer, negotiate by phone, fax or email: contact all dealerships in the area, provide specifics on the car you want, and ask for their best price. This strategy puts *you* in control, and eliminates the pressure of the sales floor!

326 Don't buy a status car

A car is a means of transportation from Point A to Point B. It's not—as marketers would have you believe—a symbol of your success, reflection of your personality, or expression of your innermost soul! Don't fall victim to fancy advertising— a "designer" car can be a real drain on your bank account. Not only do luxury vehicles have higher price tags, they're more expensive to service, maintain and insure. And they're also more likely to be stolen! Instead of wasting your hard-earned dollars on a hood ornament, purchase the least expensive, most reliable car for your needs.

327 Buy a used car

New cars depreciate rapidly in their first few years—save all that money by buying a used one instead! Browse listings in the classifieds, on Craigslist.com, or on specialty sites like AutoTrader.com. When you find a prospect, order a CARFAX report on its VIN number to check the title, accident history and insurance claims. If possible, take it for a test drive, or have a mechanic look it over, before you buy. You can also purchase a pre-owned car through a dealership: most automakers sell "certified" used cars that have been thoroughly inspected and repaired. You'll even receive a warranty!

328 Mind those mpgs

Choose a car with good gas mileage, and you'll reap the rewards for years to come! If you're shopping for a vehicle, make fuel efficiency a top priority. Check the mpg rating of the car you're considering, to see how many miles you can drive on a single gallon of gas. With this information (and some details on your driving habits), online calculators can help you forecast the monthly, or yearly, gasoline expense. They'll even show you how much you'll save by choosing a more fuel-efficient model. At today's gas prices, high mpg ratings are sexier than spoilers and sunroofs!

329 Pay cash for your car

If you have extra savings earning low interest, consider paying cash for your car. You'll save thousands of dollars in finance charges, and be able to negotiate a better deal! Think you can't afford it? Make your car fit your budget, not the other way around: if you don't have the dough for a brand new convertible, settle for a used sedan. If you must take out a loan, shop around; local banks and credit unions often have cheaper rates than car dealerships. To minimize finance charges, make the largest down payment possible, and get the shortest term you can afford.

330 Drive your car forever

Buying a car is a blow to your bank account; avoid the financial impact by driving your current one as long as possible. High-mileage vehicles can be more expensive to maintain; but it's cheaper to shell out $1500 for a repair, than $15,000 for a replacement! The higher depreciation, insurance and financing costs of a new car are even more reasons to keep your old one going. To lengthen the life of your auto, give it good care and drive it only when necessary: skip the long road trips, take public transit when possible, and do local errands on foot or by bike.

331 Consider insurance costs

When shopping for your next car, factor into your decision the cost of insurance—this recurring charge will affect your finances for years after the purchase. Narrow your selection to a couple of vehicles, then contact your insurance agent (or go online) to obtain rate quotes for each candidate. Premiums can vary widely, depending on the make, model and year of the car. If all else is equal, choose the one that's cheapest to insure. In your quest to be a frugillionaire, you may have to forgo that red Italian roadster—but you'll have a bigger bank account to bolster your ego!

332 Shop around for car insurance

Put your shopping skills to use, and find the best deal on car insurance! It may not be as fun as buying a new handbag or stereo system—but it's significantly more rewarding. And it's not as hard as it sounds: all you need is a computer, and a few minutes of spare time. Type "car insurance" into your favorite search engine, and you'll get links to all the major insurers. Most provide instant online quotes after you fill in a short questionnaire. To save even more time, try an independent site such as Insurance.com, which lets you compare rates from multiple companies with a single online form.

333 Review your car insurance

Periodically review your car insurance—recent changes in lifestyle and driving habits can mean reduced rates. If you've gotten married in the past year, entered into middle age, or improved your credit rating, you may be eligible for lower premiums. A shorter commute, garage parking, or recent move to a "safer" neighborhood can also net you some savings. When it's time to renew your policy, check competitors' rates to make sure you're getting a good deal. Go directly to each company's website, or use an independent site to compare offerings.

334 Choose a higher deductible

Lower the cost of your car insurance by choosing a higher deductible. The deductible is how much money you must pay out of pocket, after an accident, before your coverage kicks in. Amounts typically range from $100 to $2000—the higher the deductible, the lower your premium. Before you raise yours, make sure you have enough cash in an emergency fund to cover the higher amount. Understand that if you have a $1000 deductible, and your car suffers $800 in damage, you'll have to pay the entire expense. But if the insurance savings are substantial (as they often are), it can be worth it!

335 Drop extra coverage on older cars

Drop collision and comprehensive coverage on older cars, and save a bundle on insurance premiums. Collision coverage pays for damage when your car hits, or is hit by, another vehicle. Comprehensive coverage is for non-collision damage like theft, vandalism, fire and severe weather. Buying these options may not make sense if your car is older, paid in full, and has a low resale value—because the insurance company won't pay for damages exceeding your car's value. For example, if your car's only worth $1000—and you have a $1000 deductible—don't pay for this extra coverage, as you won't receive any compensation.

336 Consolidate insurance policies

Insure all of your family's cars on the same policy, and you'll likely receive a multiple vehicle discount. The savings can be significant—up to 25 percent—so be sure to ask your agent about it. Most companies also offer multi-line policy discounts: you'll qualify for a reduced rate if you buy both your automobile and homeowner's (or renter's) insurance from the same firm. In fact, the more business you do with a particular insurer, the more you'll be rewarded; therefore, you may want to consider consolidating life, business and liability policies as well.

337 Ask about insurance discounts

Insurance companies offer various discounts on automobile policies—find out which ones you qualify for! If you haven't had an accident or moving violation in the last three years, you may be eligible for a good driver's discount. Garaging your car, installing an anti-theft device, and driving a car with certain safety features—like airbags and antilock brakes—can also win you lower rates. Some insurers will reduce your premium if you etch your car's VIN number on the windows. For additional savings, inquire about group discounts for any organizations you belong to, and encourage teenage drivers in your household to get good grades!

338 Don't pay for unnecessary coverage

Review your car insurance policy carefully, to make sure you're not paying for unnecessary coverage. Drop those options you'll likely never use, or could afford to pay out of pocket. You may not need towing coverage, for example, if you belong to the American Automobile Association (AAA), or if your new car includes roadside assistance under the warranty. Does your policy include coverage for car rental costs? Pass on this option if you have a second car you can use—or access to other transportation—while your vehicle is in the repair shop.

339 Avoid installment fees

Save money by paying your entire insurance premium at once. Most companies charge a service fee for dividing the total cost of a policy (which typically covers a six or twelve month period) into monthly installments. These fees can add several dollars to each payment. If you can afford it, pay your premium in full to avoid this extra cost. Alternatively, ask if your insurer offers an automatic bank draft program. Installment fees may be waived if you have payments deducted directly from your bank account. You'll also avoid the hassle—and cost—of writing and mailing checks!

340 Improve your credit score

Many insurers consider credit scores when calculating premiums. Fairly or not, their computerized algorithms associate higher credit ratings with lower-risk individuals. Therefore, the better your credit, the less you'll pay for coverage—and vice versa. Improve your risk profile, and save money, by working to raise your credit score. Reduce credit card balances, and always pay bills on time—just one late payment can damage your rating. Open new accounts only as needed, and check your credit report regularly for errors. Manage your money like a frugillionaire, and you'll be rewarded with lower premiums!

341 Drive safely

An accident, speeding ticket or other moving violation can put a huge dent in your bank account! Not only will you have to pay the fines incurred—you'll also be hit with higher insurance rates. Avoid financial (and physical) pain by driving with caution, and obeying all traffic rules. Don't tailgate, speed, or run red lights; and don't drive when drowsy, drunk, or otherwise impaired. Refrain from distractions—like eating, texting, or talking on a cell phone—while behind the wheel. Go one step further, and take a defensive driving course; you'll learn valuable techniques for accident prevention, and may receive an insurance discount!

Chapter 10

TRAVEL

Roaming the World
without a Trust Fund

---

342 Be your own travel agent

Take charge of your travel plans, and cut out the middleman! With an internet connection, and a little legwork, you can save a bundle on fees and commissions. Travel websites— like Orbitz.com, Expedia.com and Hotels.com—help you find the lowest prices on flights, car rentals and accommodations. Type in your dates and destination, and see what deals they have to offer. Be certain to read the fine print, and understand the cancellation policies, of special rates and packages. For best results, check out online reviews by fellow travelers before booking a hotel, cruise or tour.

343 Plan well in advance

Plan your trip well in advance to secure the lowest airfare—especially if your travel dates aren't flexible! Try to purchase your ticket at least three weeks before departure; the price can rise exponentially in the days leading up to the flight. Reserve international flights even earlier; they're more limited in number, and fill up quickly during popular travel times. If the fare drops in the meantime, some airlines will reissue your ticket and give you a credit voucher for future travel. Such refund policies are usually not advertised, so check your carrier's website, or call their customer service line, for details.

344 Be flexible with your plans

Frugillionaires score big savings by being flexible with their travel plans! Check the fares for the two days before, and after, your ideal departure date; the difference in cost may surprise you. Some travel websites let you search for flights in a multi-day window, making it easy to plan both legs when the fares are cheapest. You can also get a lower ticket price by flying on less popular days, and during less popular times—like a Wednesday night at 11:00 pm. And if you're willing to make a connection or two, you can save hundreds of dollars over flying direct!

345 Find last-minute bargains

If you're *really* flexible, take advantage of last-minute bargains. In order to fill their flights, airlines release empty seats—at rock bottom prices—a few days before departure. You'll save lots of money if you can leave at a moment's notice! Find these frugal fares on airline and travel websites, or sign up for email notifications to get them delivered to your inbox. For extra fun, let the price determine your destination: grab the cheapest flight, and have a spontaneous weekend in the city where it terminates! Search the web, and you'll also find last-minute vacation packages, complete with accommodations.

346 Use alternate airports

When you book a flight, don't automatically choose the largest airport in the area (or the one closest to home) as your point of departure. You can often find less expensive fares by broadening your search. Check the cost of flying out of *all* the airports in your region; it may be cheaper to leave from one that's smaller, or in another city. If this change of itinerary requires a train ride, longer drive, or additional parking expense, consider these factors when comparing airfares. All else being equal, the savings may be worth a little inconvenience!

347 Sign up for email alerts

Sign up for email alerts, and be the first to know about special travel deals! Why waste time searching for bargains, when they can be sent straight to your inbox? Register with the websites of major airlines and hotel chains, to receive automatic notifications of low fares and special rates. Sites like Travelocity.com and Expedia.com let you specify destinations of interest, and contact you when great deals come up on airfare, accommodations and vacation packages for those places. It's like having your own travel concierge, absolutely free of charge!

348 Book a package

Sometimes buying a vacation package—that includes both airfare and accommodations—yields greater savings than booking your flight and hotel separately. Keep an eye on travel websites: aggregators combine vacant seats with vacant rooms, and sell them together at deeply discounted rates. Check with airlines as well; they often partner with hotels for special promotions. Some packages even include car rental and admission to popular tourist attractions. Just remember, the best bargains are for last-minute departures; so have your bags packed and be ready to go!

349 Gamble for your room

Use blind-booking sites like Priceline.com and Hotwire.com to get great deals on hotel rooms. This is one situation in which a little gambling can really pay off! Hotwire lets you know the class, location and price of available rooms: for example, a four-star hotel in Times Square for $199 per night. You won't find out the name of the hotel until *after* you book it. Priceline operates similarly, but also allows you to make an offer: choose the hotel class and location, and name the price you're willing to pay. If your offer is accepted, the reservation is made, and the details of the hotel are revealed. If you're flexible, it's a fun and frugal way to find a room!

350 Don't follow the crowd

When it comes to travel, it pays to march to a different drummer! To save money, frugillionaires go where the crowds aren't. Hotels in major cities are most expensive during the week, when they cater to business travelers. Book your stay for the weekend instead; prices are slashed when the road warriors clear out. Resorts, on the other hand, attract a Friday through Sunday crowd; plan your visit mid-week for much lower rates. Get the best airfare deals by flying at unpopular times, like late weekday nights or early Saturday morning. You'll also have a better choice of seats!

351 Travel in the off-season

Get huge discounts on flights, accommodations and vacation packages, by traveling in the off-season. During slow periods, airlines and hotels slash prices to fill vacant seats and empty rooms. Take advantage of their desperation, and save 50 percent or more off the regular cost. If possible, avoid traveling during holidays and summer breaks, when you'll pay peak rates; try the less expensive "shoulder" seasons, like September/October and March/April, instead. Vacation in the dead of winter for even greater savings. As an added bonus, museums and tourist sites will be free of crowds—and may even offer reduced admission!

352 Take day trips

Airfare and hotel rooms take the biggest bite out of your vacation budget. Eliminate these expenses, by taking day trips instead! Fabulous travel doesn't have to involve far-flung destinations; look in your own region for interesting attractions. Explore nearby sites of historical significance; visit museums, zoos and botanical gardens; or take a hike on a wilderness trail. Consult a map for ideas—an hour or two's drive may put you in a vibrant city, a lakefront resort or a national park. Alternatively, take a bus or train to your destination; fares are usually quite reasonable, and you can relax en route!

353 Commune with nature

Forget the pricey resorts, fancy restaurants, and overpriced theme parks—commune with nature instead! National and state parks are easy on the budget: admission is generally inexpensive, and sometimes even free of charge. The experience, however, is priceless: you'll enjoy pristine beaches, lush forests, miles of hiking trails and spectacular views. Pack a picnic lunch, and enjoy it in a gorgeous natural setting. For a longer getaway, camp for a few nights under the stars; you can bring your own tent, or rent a cabin at very reasonable rates. It's more frugal—and fun—than booking a hotel room!

354 Sign up for loyalty programs

Stretch your travel dollars further—by being a loyal customer! If you use a particular airline regularly, sign up for its frequent flyer program. You'll earn a certain number of points for every mile you travel. These credits accumulate in your account, and can be exchanged for tickets, upgrades and other rewards. Chain hotels offer similar programs, rewarding frequent stays with a free night. Read terms and conditions carefully, and understand the rules and restrictions for redeeming your points. For tips on getting maximum value from loyalty plans, check out websites like FrequentFlier.com and FlyerTalk.com.

355 Get a travel rewards card

Sign up for a credit card that rewards you with travel miles. Whenever you make a purchase, you'll earn points toward airfare, hotel stays and car rentals. Just imagine: every bag of groceries, and gallon of gas, will get you a little closer to that Hawaiian vacation! Read the fine print carefully when selecting a card. Ideally, choose one with no annual fee, and minimal blackout dates and restrictions. These cards often have high interest rates, so pay off the balance in full each month; otherwise, the finance charges could exceed the value of your rewards!

356 Ask for discounts

Don't be shy—to get a discount, sometimes all you need to do is ask for it! Call the hotel in which you'd like to stay, and request a reduced rate or free extra night. Or if you arrive without a reservation, negotiate with the agent behind the counter; they're usually authorized to give lower rates at their discretion. Let them know if a competitor is offering a more attractive deal; they may match it—or better it—to get your business. Your chance of success is greater with smaller, independent hotels, but even the big ones will bend on price in order to fill vacancies.

357 Ask for upgrades

When you check into a hotel, ask for an upgrade—it only takes a minute, and the worst they'll say is no. On the other hand, you may secure a larger room or an ocean view! It helps to arrive late in the day; if suites are still unoccupied, clerks are more likely to give them away. Be pleasant and polite when making your request, and let them know if you're celebrating a special occasion. Use the same strategy when flying: ask the counter agent for an upgrade to business or first class. If seats are available, your wish may be granted, especially if you're a frequent flyer with the airline.

358 Use membership discounts

Do you belong to the AAA, AARP or other national organization? If so, make sure you tell the ticket agent when making travel reservations! Membership in certain groups can garner discounts on hotel rooms, car rentals and admission to tourist attractions. Many hotels also offer special rates for military personnel, government employees and those who work in the travel industry; be prepared to show proper identification when checking in. If you're a business traveler, ask for the hotel's corporate rate; you'll usually qualify even if you're self-employed.

359 Use children's discounts

If you're traveling with little ones, take advantage of any discounts for which they're eligible! Plane seats must be purchased for children over the age of two, but most airlines offer reduced fares for pint-sized passengers. Infants can usually travel on a parent's lap for free. Many major hotel chains let kids under eighteen stay free, and some restaurants provide discounted (or complimentary) children's meals. Depending on their age, kids may also qualify for free or discounted admission to museums and tourist attractions, and lower fares on public transit.

360 Sleep under the stars

Skip the room service, and go camping—it's a budget-friendly way to visit some of the most beautiful areas of the country. Campsites are plentiful in popular destinations, and are often located just down the road from pricey resorts. Some are free, while others charge a small fee for each night you stay. Costs will depend on whether you're using a tent or recreational vehicle (RV). Don't be intimidated by the idea of "roughing" it: many sites provide amenities such as hot showers and clean restrooms, and some even have cabins, yurts and other accommodations for rent.

361 Stay in a hostel

Stretch your travel budget by staying in a hostel, instead of a hotel. In the past, hostels catered almost exclusively to young, single backpackers, providing dormitory-style accommodations and few amenities. Fortunately for frugillionaires, times have changed. Many hostels have upgraded their facilities to attract older travelers, and private rooms are often available for couples and families. There are usually full kitchens on site, which can drastically cut down your dining expenses. Best of all, hostels have common lounges where guests can socialize—affording you a wonderful opportunity to meet people from all over the world!

362 Stay in a bed and breakfast

A bed and breakfast can be a great budget alternative to a full service hotel. Rates are typically lower, and the owners more willing to negotiate them; and a full (and usually hearty!) breakfast is included in the price. B&B's range from full-size inns, to private homes with a few rooms for rent. Bathrooms may be en suite or shared with other guests. Be sure to chat with the proprietors during your visit, as they're usually wonderful sources of knowledge about the area. They'll give you advice, make recommendations, and do more to make your stay enjoyable than will most hotel concierges!

363 Stay with friends or relatives

The most frugal accommodations of all are the houses of friends and relatives. If they've invited you to stay, accept their offer—you'll save a fortune on hotel costs! Arrive with a small gift—such as fresh flowers, a fruit basket or a nice bottle of wine—as a token of your appreciation. And while you're there, remember to be a gracious houseguest: keep your room tidy, help with the cooking, and offer to do the dishes. Free lodging doesn't include maid service! After you leave, follow-up with a thank you note. Let your hosts know you enjoyed their company, and express your gratitude for their hospitality.

364 Rent a condo or house

Live like a local: rent a condominium or house on your next vacation! These accommodations are usually rented by the week or month, and can be far more economical than a full service hotel. Private homes are particularly cost-effective for families and groups, eliminating the expense of multiple hotel rooms. You'll love the convenience of having laundry facilities and a kitchen, and can save a fortune in food costs by preparing your own meals. Ask a travel agent about available options, or search online for short-term rentals. For the best deals, skip the middleman and deal directly with the owner!

365 Swap your house

Get free accommodations when you travel—by swapping your house! Borrow the home of another family, and lend them yours in return. It's easy: register online with a website like HomeExchange.com or HomeLink.org, and post photos and details of your abode. Browse through the listings in your favorite destinations, and when you spot a potential candidate, contact them and propose a swap. Meanwhile, people who see your posting may request to trade with you. Once you find a match, get to know your partner by telephone or email. Iron out the dates and details, and sign a home exchange agreement (see samples online).

366 Stay outside the city

Big, expensive cities come with big, expensive hotel prices! You'll pay a premium to stay in the center of the action. Consider a hotel on the outskirts instead, about 10-15 minutes from the downtown; rates will be significantly lower. Just make sure transportation costs won't wipe out your savings. Accommodations on a public transit line—with bus, train, trolley or subway service—are ideal. Even taking taxi rides into the city may be more cost-effective than lodging there. If possible, avoid locations that necessitate car rental; it's a hassle to drive, and expensive to park, in most major cities.

367 Use hotel shuttle services

Make use of your hotel's shuttle service to save money on transportation! Don't shell out big bucks for a taxi to the airport; many hotels run their own shuttle bus, on a regular schedule, to and from the terminals. The trip is usually free of charge for hotel guests. Some shuttles provide rides to tourist attractions as well, or run a loop through popular sights. The latter can be a great way to "tour" the area without the expense of a guide! Depending on the extent of their route, and number of stops, they can even be an alternative to public transportation.

368 Use public transit

Ride the rails—and the buses, subways, trolleys and ferries—during your next trip! Many cities are well served by public transit, and some options—like the waterbuses of Venice, and streetcars of San Francisco—are tourist attractions themselves. Familiarize yourself with the network before you reach your destination; maps are available online, in guidebooks and through tourist bureaus. Choose a hotel near a public transit stop for maximum convenience and savings. You'll eliminate the costs of taxis, rental cars and parking, and experience the city like a local!

369 Get a tourist transit pass

Riding public transit saves you money when traveling; getting a tourist pass saves you even more! As a sightseer, you'll cover much more ground than the typical commuter—and buying individual train, bus and subway tickets can add up fast. A tourist transit pass gives you unlimited rides on a city's transportation network for a certain period of time (like one day, three days or a week). They're not only cost-effective, they make navigating an unfamiliar transit system less intimidating. You won't have to worry about decoding fare schedules in foreign languages, or being caught with the wrong type of ticket!

370 Explore on foot

A frugillionaire's favorite way to experience a town or city is by walking its streets. Taxis and tourist buses are expensive, and keep you removed from the action. Make your way to restaurants, museums and tourist attractions on foot instead. Give yourself plenty of time, and take in all the sights, sounds and smells around you. Browse through the shops, grab a snack at the market, check out the newsstands and rest in the park. It's much more interesting to be part of the crowd, rather than a spectator. Plus, you'll discover all those wonderful little places you never read about in guidebooks!

371 Shop around for car rentals

When booking a rental car, shop around for the best deal. The same company may offer different rates through different sources: call their 800-number, check their website, and contact their local office to find the lowest price. Travel websites—like Expedia.com and Travelocity.com—make it quick and easy to compare offers. Simply enter your dates, pick-up location, and car preference; in an instant, you'll receive a list of rental agencies and rates. To save additional money, look for coupons and special promotions, and ask for any discounts (such as AAA or AARP) for which you qualify!

372 Be savvy about car rentals

If you rent your car at the airport, you'll usually pay a premium—check the rates at other locations before making your reservation. The savings may be worth a short trek to another facility. Compare daily and weekly rates as well; it may be more cost-effective to rent a car for the week, even if you only use it a few days. Read the fine print, and check if fees are imposed on early returns. And finally, don't forget to fill the tank before you drop the car off; most agencies charge a hefty price per gallon if you bring it back empty!

373 Don't buy unnecessary insurance

When you rent a car, think twice before taking the extra insurance—it may be unnecessary. Rental vehicles are often covered under personal auto policies; check yours, or contact your agent, for details. You may also receive coverage for collision and theft if you pay for the car with your credit card. On the other hand, you may be better off with the rental agent's insurance if you have a high deductible on your own policy, if an accident would increase your premium, or if you're renting in a foreign country. To make the most cost-effective choice, do your homework *before* arriving at the rental counter!

374 Use ATMs for foreign currency

When you're traveling abroad, don't lose a fortune converting your dollars! Exchange desks are known for unfavorable rates and high commissions; and changing money at hotels, restaurants and retail stores will cost you even more. Instead, use ATM machines for your foreign currency needs. They charge a fair exchange rate, and are widely available in most towns and cities. To minimize bank charges, use no-fee ATMs whenever possible, and withdraw the maximum amount allowed. Just be sure to wear a money belt, so you'll have a secure place to stash your cash.

375 Make exchange rates work in your favor

The current exchange rate can have a huge impact on your vacation budget! When the dollar is strong, overseas travel is a bargain; your money goes further when shopping, dining and booking hotels. A weak dollar, on the other hand, will give you a serious case of sticker shock. When planning your next trip, make exchange rates work in your favor. If the dollar is weak against the Euro, but strong against the Argentine peso, skip Barcelona and head to Buenos Aires! You can also come out ahead (when the dollar is falling) by booking prepaid cruises and vacation packages.

376 Read travelers' reviews online

To get the most bang for your travel buck, get tips from fellow tourists! You'll find thousands of independent reviews—on hotels, restaurants, attractions and more—on websites like TripAdvisor.com and TripConnect.com. The advice is more honest and helpful than anything you'll read in a travel brochure. If you have specific questions, post them to the public forums; you'll receive answers from experienced travelers and in-the-know locals. Do your research beforehand, and you'll be less likely to waste your money on a bad meal, a dumpy room, or an overpriced tourist trap!

377 Use coupons and passes

Look for discounts to popular tourist sites—why pay full price if you don't have to? Tourism bureaus commonly offer coupon books and vouchers for local attractions. Check their websites in advance of your trip, or visit their offices when you arrive. If you plan to do a lot of sightseeing, consider purchasing a tourist card or pass—you'll get reduced (or free) admission to museums, landmarks and other must-see spots. Rides on public transit may even be included. Be particularly vigilant for bargains in the off-season; promotional deals abound during slow periods!

378 Do things that are free

Pass on pricey tourist traps, and do things that are free—the best travel experiences don't require admission! Strolling the streets of an unfamiliar city can be more interesting, and enjoyable, than shuffling through stuffy museums. Admire the art and architecture of local churches, and browse shops and boutiques to see regional handicrafts. If you're in a foreign country, pop into a grocery store; wandering the aisles can be quite entertaining! For more laid-back sightseeing, hang out in parks and plazas where locals congregate, and just sit back and take in the scene!

379 Pack light

The happy traveler's best secret is packing light! Nothing ruins a vacation faster than having to drag around a heavy suitcase—or pay extra fees for it at the airport check-in. Some airlines assess hefty charges for excess, or overweight, luggage. Save money by bringing just one bag, and packing only the essentials. Choose versatile clothing that works from daytime to dinner, and plan to wear each piece a few times. A clothesline and small packet of detergent take up much less space than a full wardrobe. With minimal baggage, you'll feel footloose, fancy free, and ready for anything!

380 Chat with the locals

Instead of paying for a tour guide, frugillionaires ask locals for advice! Most residents are happy to help out visitors, and will embrace the chance to wax poetic on the charms of their hometown. Inquire about their favorite places to eat, drink and hang out. Chances are, you'll come away from the exchange with invaluable knowledge: like where to find the liveliest nightlife, best slice of pizza, or first-rate espresso. Recommendations by those in the know will usually be reasonably priced and filled with locals—making for an authentic, budget-friendly experience!

381 Download walking tours

Taking a walking tour is a wonderful way to explore a new city—and all the information you need is available free of charge on the internet! Type the name of the city and "walking tour" into your favorite search engine, and you'll find plenty of itineraries from which to choose. They map specific routes to walk, and provide information on the sights you'll see along the way. Print out a copy to take with you on your trip. You can also download audio tours, and listen to them on your iPod or mp3 player as you explore your destination; it's like having your own personal guide!

382 Check out local event listings

For frugal fun while traveling, add some local flavor to your itinerary! Most cities publish a weekly paper with entertainment listings, cultural activities and other happenings in the area. Many events are free of charge—and free of tourists! Consider yourself lucky if there's a fair, festival or farmers' market in town; you'll be able to experience the culture of the region, and enjoy some interesting (and inexpensive) street food. In the evenings, look beyond the hotel bar for nightlife: attend a poetry reading in a French coffeehouse, an outdoor movie in an Italian piazza, or a concert in a Viennese church!

383 Pack your own snacks

When traveling by car, plane or train, save a bundle by bringing your own snacks! Concession stands at airports, and café cars on trains, charge hefty premiums for their items. A granola bar, or bag of chips, can cost double the grocery store price. And don't count on getting free food in-flight; some airlines now make you pay for your peanuts! Fill your carry-on bag with your own fare—like crackers, sandwiches and protein bars—and eliminate this extra expense. Use a similar strategy on road trips: instead of stopping at mini-marts, stock up on munchies before starting out!

384 Visit the grocery store

Put the local grocery store at the top of your travel itinerary, and you'll save big bucks over the course of your vacation. Stock up on fruit, snacks and beverages for your hotel room; include perishables if you have a small refrigerator or kitchenette. You'll be much less likely to raid the mini-bar and rack up sky-high charges! If in a weak moment you consume a $6 box of candy, run to the store and try to replace it before the hotel staff notices. But be forewarned: the latest mini-bar technology uses infrared sensors, and automatically bills your room the instant an item is removed!

385 Picnic

Dining out can put a huge dent in your travel budget; save some money by having picnics! Visit the local market to assemble your meal. Fruit, bagels and yogurt are a frugal alternative to a breakfast buffet, while sandwich fixings—like bread, cheese, smoked salmon or sliced meats—make a satisfying lunch. Browse the prepared foods section for a budget-friendly dinner. After you've purchased your picnic fare, find a picturesque place to enjoy it. Take the opportunity to eat al fresco in the shadow of a famous landmark—like the Eiffel Tower, Roman Coliseum, or Statue of Liberty. It's less expensive, and a lot more fun, than sitting in a stuffy restaurant!

386 Dine out at lunch

If you like to try out restaurants when you travel, visit them for lunch instead of dinner! Since midday menus are usually similar to (but less expensive than) evening versions, it's a great way to sample the culinary delights of a region without blowing your budget. Many establishments even offer lunch specials, where you'll get a two- or three-course meal, with beverage, at a fixed price. Furthermore, there's just something fabulous about having a long, luxurious lunch in the middle of a workday; it really makes you appreciate being on vacation!

387 Take a "staycation"

Avoid the long lines at airport security, by taking a "staycation." Spend your time off in the luxury of your own home: sleep late, linger over the newspaper, and take long bubble baths. Get bagels, muffins and pastries, and make your own breakfast buffet. Explore your hometown with the eyes and enthusiasm of a tourist: admire the architecture, browse through the shops, visit the museums, and dine in the restaurants. If you're feeling outdoorsy, pitch a tent and camp out in the backyard. A "staycation" will save you a bundle in travel costs—and you won't have to worry about what to pack!

Chapter 11

FINANCE

Managing Your Money and Making it Grow

---

388 Don't buy what you can't afford

It's the simplest advice in the world, but has a powerful effect on your personal finances: don't buy what you can't afford. Write it down, commit it to memory, and say it over and over again when you're out shopping. There's nothing fabulous about being in debt, or struggling to make payments on an impulse purchase. The pleasure of acquiring that new dress, sofa or television quickly fades when you have to find a way to pay for it. The next time you're tempted by a shiny new what's-it, take control of the situation. Instead of pulling out the credit card, wait until you have the cash in the bank to pay for it!

389 Flash the cash

To hold onto more of your hard-earned dollars, cut up your credit cards and use only cash. This frugillionaire strategy will save you a bundle in finance charges, and put the brakes on your shopping habit—because without credit, you can't spend more than the money you have. Paying with plastic is far too painless. Since the bill doesn't come until the end of the month, it feels like you're getting something for free. Paying with cash, on the other hand, makes the transaction more "real." When you have to hand over good old greenbacks, you may think twice before making the purchase!

390 Don't hang out at the mall

If you're trying to save money, don't hang out at the mall—the temptation is just too great! What's so exciting about wandering through racks of clothing, or shelves of electronics, anyway? It does nothing for your mental or physical well-being, and can be downright dangerous to your finances. Instead of frequenting retail stores in your leisure time, go to the park, art museum, or local coffee shop. Get involved in community activities, volunteer for a good cause, or spend the afternoon with friends and family. You'll have a fuller wallet, and a more interesting life!

391 Freeze your credit cards – literally

If you're reluctant to cut up your credit cards—in case you need one to rent a car, reserve a hotel room, or address a true emergency—try freezing them instead. Fill a small container with water, immerse the card(s) inside, and place it in the freezer. In short order, your plastic will be trapped in a block of ice—and safely out of reach if you're heading to the mall, or shopping on the internet! This technique saves you money by putting a damper on impulse purchases. When you feel the desire to make one, you'll have to wait a few hours for the card to thaw; with any luck, the urge to splurge will melt away in the meantime!

392 Keep a spending diary

If you wonder where your money goes, start a spending diary. Record every purchase you make, along with the price, in a notebook or computer spreadsheet. Include *every expenditure*, no matter how small or insignificant it seems—those bridge tolls, magazines, and bottles of water add up! Divide expenses into categories (so you can pinpoint problem areas), and calculate your totals at the end of each month. You'll quickly learn where you need to cut back. In fact, you may even find yourself spending less—to avoid the hassle of writing it down!

393 Be a borrower of things, not money

It's always better to borrow an item, than borrow the money to buy it! Whether you need a sewing machine or a circular saw, refrain from running to the store—ask family members if they have one to lend. Instead of buying extra plates for your upcoming dinner party, borrow some from your next-door neighbor. And if you'd like to film a special event, don't put a camcorder on your credit card—see if a friend will let you use theirs. Return all items in good condition, and be equally generous with your own possessions. Remember: borrowing money *costs* money, while borrowing things *saves* it!

394 Go on a spending fast

Select a specific time period—like a day, week, or month—and go on a spending fast. During this time, don't buy anything but necessities, like basic food and toiletries. Find creative ways to meet your needs, and make do with the things you already have. You'll be amazed how much money you save, simply by staying out of the stores! In fact, you may even feel a sense of relief when you're not "allowed" to shop. As your resolve builds, try a more ambitious challenge: refrain from buying particular items—such as new clothes, housewares, or electronic gadgets—for an entire year!

395 Join groups for support

When you're trying to kick a spending habit, turn to others for support. Seek out local discussion groups on your topic of interest—be it voluntary simplicity, financial planning, debt reduction, cost-cutting, or recovering from a shopping addiction. Consult Meetup.com, or community bulletin boards, to find meetings in your area. Alternatively, search for support on the internet. Online discussion forums on personal finance and frugality—like SimpleLiving.net and GetRichSlowly.org—connect you with kindred souls. Post messages, reply to others, and find strength and inspiration in the virtual camaraderie!

396 Save up for what you want

Save up for your next big purchase, instead of buying it on credit. Whether it's a new car, a dishwasher or a designer handbag, make do without it until you have the cash. Don't pay interest for instant gratification! When you figure in finance charges, you're actually overpaying for the item—just for the privilege of having it immediately. Instead, wait until you've accumulated the money in the bank; it may take weeks, months or even years. By that time, you may not even want the item anymore; and in that case, you can congratulate yourself on how much you saved!

397 Know your net worth

Know your net worth—it's the key to taking control of your finances, and becoming a frugillionaire. Sit down and do the math: your net worth is simply your assets (what you own) minus your liabilities (what you owe). Add up all your cash, stock, bonds, certificates of deposit and other liquid assets, as well as the current value of any real estate or vehicles you own. Subtract from that amount all your debts: mortgages, car loans, student loans, home equity loans, consumer loans and credit card balances. The resulting figure is your net worth. Ideally, it should be positive—and the bigger the better!

398 Mind your net worth

Consumption is the number one obstacle to preserving, and growing, your net worth; keep this in mind when considering a purchase! Each time you buy something, you have to draw down your savings (decrease your assets) or take out a loan (increase your liabilities) to pay for it— sacrificing some of your net worth in the process. Ask yourself if that $150 cashmere sweater, or $5000 home theater system, is worth the negative hit to your finances—or the effort it'll take to climb back out of the hole. You may decide that it's more gratifying to have a bigger bank account, than the item under consideration!

399 Pay yourself first

To keep more of your paycheck, pay yourself first! Your savings should come off the top of your earnings, not from what's left over. Pick an arbitrary amount—say 10 percent of your income—and put it in the bank, or 401(k) account, each month. Treat it as another bill that simply *must* be paid—on par with your rent, utilities, taxes and insurance premiums. Better yet, make it automatic: set up direct deposit to move the funds straight into savings. If you never see the money, you won't be able to spend it; it's a simple, painless way to achieve financial security!

400 Enroll in a 401(k) plan

Join your company's 401(k) plan—and have plenty of green for your golden years! Once enrolled, request to have a portion of each paycheck deposited directly into your 401(k) account. You won't have to pay taxes on this money—or what you earn from investing it—until you withdraw it at retirement. As an added bonus, your company may match your contributions: meaning that for every dollar you put into your account, your employer may add another dollar, up to a certain percent of your income. These matching funds are free money—so contribute enough to get the maximum amount!

401 Consider a Roth IRA

Consider opening a Roth IRA; it's another way to save for when you're old and gray! A Roth IRA differs from traditional retirement accounts in several ways. Most importantly: your contributions are not tax-deductible like a 401(k), but your money can be withdrawn tax-free at retirement age. In other words, instead of getting your tax break sooner (when you contribute your money), you get it later (when you withdraw it). Therefore, as long as certain rules are met, the investment *earnings* in a Roth IRA will never be taxed! Consult your accountant for complete details, and to determine the best savings strategy for your personal situation.

402 Invest in index funds

Stock-picking is hard work; who has the time, and inclination, to pore over balance sheets and quarterly reports? Even professionals have a hard time choosing winners: the vast majority of mutual funds underperform the overall market. Invest in index funds instead; they get rid of the guesswork, and give you instant diversification over a wide range of stocks. Index funds are designed to mirror the movement of an entire market, like the S&P 500; so if the market goes up, you make money! Furthermore, because they use a buy and hold strategy, their fees are much lower than regular mutual funds—providing an extra boost to your returns!

403 Use an online discount broker

Trade stocks, bonds and mutual funds online; you'll forgo the advice of a full-service broker, but save a fortune in commissions and fees! This do-it-yourself method is particularly cost-effective for small, straightforward transactions—like purchasing 100 shares of XYZ stock. Many discount brokers even provide access to reports and research tools, to help you make more-informed decisions. One word of caution: don't automatically choose the broker with the lowest fee-per-trade. Inquire about account maintenance fees, and find out if you must maintain a minimum balance (or make a certain number of trades) to qualify for discounted rates.

404 Automate your investments

Don't try to time the market—automate your investments instead! Dollar-cost averaging is a simple technique, in which you buy a fixed dollar amount of a certain investment on a regular schedule. For example, you can set up your brokerage account to buy $100 of a certain index fund every month. Your money buys more shares when the price is low, and fewer when the price is high. This strategy smoothes out the effects of market volatility on your portfolio. And because it's automatic, it keeps you from making emotional investment decisions—like being "afraid" to buy when the share price is falling, or buying too much when the market is high.

405 Buy municipal bonds

Save money at tax time by investing in municipal bonds or bond funds. Municipal bonds are debt obligations (IOU's) issued by state or local governments, usually to raise money for public projects. Unlike corporate bonds, the interest earned on municipal bonds is exempt from federal taxes. And if the bond is issued by the state in which you live, you won't have to pay state taxes on it either! To decide whether you're better off buying taxable or municipal bonds, you'll have to consider both the yield of the bond and your tax bracket. Speak with your accountant, or search online for further details.

406 Sign up for an online bank account

Earn more interest by banking online! The interest on traditional checking accounts ranges from little to none; after all, banks must maintain those marble lobbies, and pay tellers to handle your transactions. Online checking accounts eliminate that overhead, and therefore offer much higher rates. With an online account, you can pay your bills and check your balances with a click of the mouse; deposits and withdrawals are made through the mail or an ATM. You can also establish an electronic link between your online and traditional accounts, and easily transfer money between them.

407 Avoid overdraft fees

Banks charge big fees when you overdraw your account; avoid them with good record keeping. Write every transaction—check, deposit, withdrawal or debit card purchase—in your register as it occurs. When your bank statement arrives each month, double check all entries against your checkbook and make sure the balances match. When you know exactly how much money you have, you're much less likely to bounce a check! Online banking services make it even easier to stay up-to-date on account activity: you can check your balances regularly, and set up email alerts to notify you when they fall below a certain amount.

408 Avoid ATM fees

Use ATMs like a frugillionaire, and save a bundle in transaction fees! Always use your own bank's machines when making a withdrawal; otherwise, you could be hit with heavy charges. Keep this in mind when opening an account, and choose a bank that has (or belongs to) a large ATM network—preferably one with machines where you live, work and shop. If you don't have access to a free ATM, reduce your number of withdrawals (and the accompanying fees) by taking out a large amount of cash each time. Alternatively, ask for cash back when making purchases with your debit card.

409 Pay bills online

Paying bills online is not only convenient—it's also cheaper! You'll save primarily on postage costs; that handful of stamps each month adds up over the course of a year. You'll also reduce (or eliminate) your need to buy checks from the bank, and envelopes in which to send them. Furthermore, online payments are faster and more reliable. They won't get lost or delayed in the mail, meaning less chance of late fees and penalties. You can even set up your account to pay recurring bills—like your mortgage, car payments and utilities—automatically. That way, you'll never run the risk of forgetting one!

410 Don't carry a balance

Shore up your finances by paying your credit card bill in full each month. When you charge an item and carry a balance, whatever you buy costs a whole lot more: you'll not only owe the purchase price, but also all the interest! As finance charges accumulate, you'll sink even deeper into debt— making it increasingly difficult, if not impossible, to get your head above water. To avoid this terrible fate: never put anything on a credit card unless you can pay off the balance at the end of the month. Then instead of drowning in debt, you can focus on building your wealth!

411 Ask for a lower interest rate

Call your credit card company, and ask them to lower your interest rate. You'll save hundreds (if not thousands) of dollars in finance charges; and the lower the rate, the faster you'll be able to pay off your debt. All it takes is a phone call, and a few minutes of your time. The worst they can say is no—and if they do, try again in a few months. You'll have a better chance of success if you have a good credit history, and have been making payments on time. Tell them you're thinking of transferring your balance to another card; they may grant your request in order to keep your business.

412 Shop for a lower interest rate

Take advantage of the competition among credit card companies, and shop around for a lower interest rate. With a lower rate, you'll pay less for financed items, and speed up debt reduction. The savings can be well worth the time and research. But beware of low introductory rates that are valid for only six to twelve months; if you can't pay off your balance in that time, make sure you know the rates at expiration. If you're aggressively paying down your debt, keep an eye out for 0% interest balance transfer offers. When you're not paying interest, *all* of your payment reduces your balance—making your debt disappear much faster!

413 Say no to annual fees

Don't carry credit cards with annual fees; it's like throwing your money away! Banks make enough profit on finance charges; you shouldn't have to pay for the "privilege" of using their card. They'll promise you perks, prestige and priority service, but chances are, you won't get enough of these "extras" to make it worthwhile. Be especially careful with rewards and low-interest rate cards, as a yearly charge can completely wipe out any benefits. If you have a card with an annual fee, call up the bank and ask them to waive it—they'll often concede, to keep you as a customer.

414 Get a rewards credit card

A rewards credit card can be a boon to your budget—if used wisely! You can earn travel points and airline miles, get discounts at your favorite stores, save money on gas, and receive cash back on your purchases. But if the promise of rewards entices you to spend more—or if you already carry a balance—forget it! Rewards cards often have high interest rates, so finance charges would erase your benefits. To come out ahead: choose one with no annual fee, use it only for purchases you would have made anyway, and pay off the balance in full each month.

415 Maintain a good credit record

When it comes to borrowing, you'll save a lot of money if you have a good credit score: the higher your rating, the lower the interest rates you'll obtain on your loans. Maintain a good history by managing your finances responsibly: don't bounce checks, overdraw your accounts, or exceed your credit limits. And most importantly, always pay your bills on time. Companies report missed and late payments directly to credit bureaus, so send at least the minimum amount if you can't pay in full. If you ignore your electric bill, for example, it'll cost you more to finance a car!

416 Monitor your credit report

Your credit report affects your borrowing costs—so monitor it regularly! Collection agencies and credit bureaus make mistakes; it's not uncommon for someone else's mortgage, or delinquent payment, to show up under *your* name. Worse yet, you may be a victim of identity theft; the faster you discover it, the less damage will be done. Each of the three main reporting bureaus—Equifax, Experian, and TransUnion—are required by law to provide you with a free annual credit report. Obtain yours on the internet at www.annualcreditreport.com, or by calling 1-877-322-8228. Spread your requests over the course of the year to keep a close eye on your records.

417 Evaluate your tax withholding

It may *feel* fabulous to get a big tax refund—but it's not fabulous to give Uncle Sam an interest-free loan! That money should be working for *you* all year instead: earning you interest, buying your gas, purchasing your groceries, and paying off your debt. If you get a big check at tax time, consider reducing your withholding—that's the percentage taken out of your paycheck each month and sent to the Internal Revenue Service. To change it, submit a new Form W-4 to your employer. Use the worksheets that accompany the form, or the withholding calculator at www.irs.gov, to compute the correct amount.

418 Bank your bonus or raise

Getting a raise is a wonderful thing; suddenly you're making more money for working the same amount of hours! It can be tempting to splurge on a coveted item, or increase your standard of living: perhaps you have your sights set on a nicer car, a bigger house or a dream vacation. But consider this: instead of acting richer, *be* richer. Bank your bonus instead of running out to spend it. Let it earn interest, and generate even more wealth. With each raise in pay, increase your financial security instead of your spending—and you'll be on the road to a much earlier retirement!

419 Build wealth with windfalls

Sometimes life rewards you with an unexpected windfall—like a bonus from your employer, a cash gift from a relative, or a tax refund from Uncle Sam; a lottery winning, an inheritance, or a rebate; or a $20 bill you find on the sidewalk. No matter what the source of these windfalls, open a separate bank account to collect them. Instead of spending this "found" money, use it to pave your path to financial freedom. Dedicate the account to savings (for retirement, a house, or your children's college funds), or use it to pay off existing debt. It's an effortless way to build your wealth!

420 Start an emergency fund

Don't let unexpected expenses—or a temporary loss of income—derail your finances. Start an emergency fund: it's the frugillionaire's best defense against unforeseen repairs, medical bills and layoffs. Save enough money to cover at least three to six months of living expenses; that'll take care of small emergencies, and go a long way toward helping you with larger ones. Keep these funds in a liquid, FDIC-insured account. Such preparation can save you from having to put that new transmission—or your groceries, if you're laid off—on a credit card. Avoiding debt in such situations is the key to quick financial recovery!

Chapter 12

CHILDREN

Raising Happy Kids
on a Pint-Sized Budget

---

421 Have a baby shower

If you're expecting a child, a baby shower is a great way to acquire all the necessities — from booties to bassinet — without breaking the bank. It's usually organized by a close friend or family member; but if you know about it in advance, don't be shy about asking for specific items. Put the emphasis on practical gifts, like a stroller, car seat, bottles and diapers; they'll be much more useful than silver spoons, stuffed animals and a closet full of cute outfits. Ideally, register for essentials with a national retailer — it's convenient for guests, prevents duplicate gifts, and guarantees you'll get exactly what you need!

422 Borrow baby items

Before you spend big bucks on a baby item—like a crib, stroller, bassinet or high chair—ask friends and family if they have one you can use. Many a playpen is stashed away in attics and basements, "just in case" another little one comes along! See if you can borrow items that are currently not in service. You can also find such products at thrift stores, yard sales, and on Craigslist.com; since they're only used for a few years, they're often in great condition. Don't compromise on safety, though; make sure all items meet current standards and regulations, and have not been subject to any recalls.

423 Furnish with what you have

It's exciting to outfit a nursery for a new arrival—but don't go broke before the baby comes! Look around your house for furnishings before you hit the stores; an unused dresser, bookshelf or table can often be pressed into service. Give the pieces a fresh coat of paint so they'll complement each other, and blend into the room. Save even more money with some DIY décor: make a mobile, sew your own curtains, or paint a cute mural on the wall. Remember, your baby will be none the wiser if his crib doesn't match his changing table; and he'll be much better off with frugillionaire parents than fancy furniture!

424 Buy multi-functional furniture

Stretch your baby budget by investing in multi-functional pieces. A convertible crib, for example, can save you money by growing along with your child. After accommodating your newborn, it transforms into a toddler bed, and later becomes a twin—eliminating the need to purchase additional furniture over the years. Just be sure to choose a classic style that your child won't outgrow. Consider other items that also do double duty: like dressers with built-in changing tables, and playpens that function as bassinets. The longer (and more often) an item is used, the better the investment!

425 Save on diapers

The price of diapers can give new parents some serious sticker shock! Buy them in bulk from warehouse and discount stores to shave a few dollars off each pack. You can also save by clipping coupons, watching sales circulars for weekly promotions, and signing up for special offers on diaper companies' websites. Consider store brands as an alternative to name brands; they're often made by the same manufacturers, but are much less expensive. And don't hesitate to ask for diapers as gifts, for your baby shower and other occasions. Grandparents, friends and relatives will be happy to oblige!

426 Use cloth diapers

Cloth diapers are gentle on your baby's bottom—and your bottom line! They've come a long way since grandma's old-fashioned prefolds, and are enjoying new popularity as an economical and eco-friendly alternative to disposables. The new generation of cloth diapers features fitted styles, Velcro strips, leak proof covers and flushable liners—greatly improving their performance, and making them easier to change, fasten and launder. Give cloth a try: the savings over disposables can be quite significant, especially if they're passed down to future siblings!

427 Breastfeed

Breastfeed your baby, and save a fortune on formula! Breast milk provides all the vitamins and nutrients your child needs, and also helps to strengthen her immune system. It can protect your baby from developing gastrointestinal problems, respiratory illnesses, ear infections and allergies (meaning less doctor bills later on). Breastfeeding may also improve your own health—from speeding weight loss, to reducing the risk of some types of cancer. If you're returning to work and can't nurse during the day, invest in a breast pump; that way, your baby can get all the benefits of your milk, with the convenience of a bottle.

428 Save on formula

Save on baby formula with some savvy shopping techniques! Join baby clubs sponsored by formula manufacturers; they'll send you free samples, and checks for their products. Buy in bulk at warehouse stores—larger sizes can substantially lower your cost per ounce. Watch the Sunday circulars for sales and coupons, and stock up when your favorite brands are discounted. Alternatively, consider generic formula; it meets the same FDA standards as name brands, but is much less expensive. You can also save by purchasing powdered versions; they're less convenient, but cheaper than ready-made.

429 Make your own baby food

Those little jars of baby food are cute and convenient—but also quite costly! Try making your own instead; it's substantially cheaper, and healthier for your tot. What's more, you can adjust the texture to suit your baby's needs, and avoid the sugar and preservatives of prepackaged fare. Fresh fruits and vegetables—like carrots, peas, sweet potatoes, apples, peaches and bananas—are economical and easy to prepare. Puree after cooking with a food processor or blender, and freeze extra portions in an ice cube tray. You'll find plenty of recipes, and detailed instructions, on the internet.

430 Flex your work schedule

Slash your day care expenses with some creative scheduling. Ask your employer if you can work flexible hours; a four-day workweek of ten-hour shifts, for example, eliminates an entire day of childcare costs. Telecommuting is another option; just be sure that you can do your job while keeping an eye on junior. If a part-time salary is sufficient, explore the possibility of job sharing (an arrangement in which one full-time position is split between two employees). You can also reduce your day care needs by staggering schedules with your spouse. These strategies not only save you money, they give you extra time with your child!

431 Ask family to babysit

If friends and family offer to babysit, take them up on it! Grandparents in particular welcome the opportunity to spend quality time with their grandchildren. Arrange for them to look after your tot one day a week while you're at work—or more often, if they're willing! Be gracious, and offer to pay for their services; if they accept compensation, it'll still be cheaper than a day care or nanny. This frugillionaire strategy is a win-win for the whole family: it saves you money on childcare costs, while giving your little one some special time with people who adore him!

432 Share a nanny

Halve the cost of a nanny—by sharing her with another family! In "share care" arrangements, a nanny tends to the children of two families at once, usually alternating between their homes on a daily or weekly basis. It's a great way to provide your child with a full-time caretaker, without having to foot the entire bill yourself. Look around your workplace or neighborhood for a partner family. Ideally, your parenting values should be similar, and your children close in age. If you have trouble finding a match, take your search online; post your request on Craigslist.com, or visit websites specializing in nanny networks.

433 Enroll your child in pre-K

If your school district has a pre-kindergarten program for three and four-year-olds, send your little scholar off to the classroom! Pre-K programs go a step beyond day care, providing activities to build physical, emotional and cognitive skills. Such early education can positively influence your child's social development and later academic achievement. Thank your lucky stars if you live in a community with full-day pre-K, as it can greatly reduce your childcare costs; even a half-day program can yield significant savings, and a smarter kid!

434 Trade babysitting services

Trade childcare duties with a friend, neighbor or family member; you'll be able to enjoy a date night with your spouse—or some quiet time alone—without the expense of a babysitter. Designate one evening a week to alternate watching each other's children: for example, you take their kids this Friday night, and they'll take yours the next. Make it a regular routine, and you'll each enjoy two "free" nights per month! You'll love being able to spend an evening out (or in the bubble bath) without having to hire a sitter; and the children will look forward to their playtime together!

435 Participate in a toy swap

When it comes to playthings, a child's short attention span can do a number on your bank account. Instead of buying another bauble, organize a toy swap with other parents. Hold a monthly get-together, to which each family brings a few gently-used toys. Put all the contributions in a play area, and let the kids make their own selections. You'll clear the house of your children's castoffs, and they'll be thrilled to get something "new!" Some communities and churches hold such events (on a larger scale) during the holidays, providing a great way to do your Christmas "shopping" without spending a dime!

436 Encourage your kids' creativity

Instead of buying more toys, engage your children in creative pursuits! Dole out paper and crayons, and provide a little instruction to get them started: ask them to draw a picture of their house, their family, their favorite animal, or what they want to be when they grow up. Encourage older children to compose songs, write stories or poems, or design dance routines. For a weekend's worth of frugal fun, help your kids (and their friends) stage a puppet show or play. Not only will they have a blast; they'll learn a variety of skills that'll serve them well beyond their childhood years!

437 Love those hand-me-downs

Kids outgrow clothing at lightning speed, so don't waste your money on pint-sized couture. Instead, use hand-me-downs from older siblings as much as possible. In fact, if you're planning to have more than one child, shop smart: skip gender-specific designs, and buy basics that'll be appropriate for a future little brother *or* sister. Supplement your child's wardrobe with thrift store finds, discount store bargains, and gently-worn donations from friends and family. Don't worry about fashion; your tykes will be much happier in thrifty threads, than fussy outfits they need to keep clean!

438 Give kids a clothing budget

When kids are old enough to choose their own attire, it can mean big trouble for your wallet. Use the opportunity to teach them fiscal responsibility—by establishing a clothing budget. Set a monthly spending limit, or make them pay for non-essentials from their allowance, gift money, or part-time job earnings. You'll be surprised how quickly they become frugal shoppers—or find creative ways to meet their needs! Your teen, for example, might decide to share clothes with a friend; they'll double their wardrobes, and have a great time swapping their fashion finds.

439 Give up the fast food

Don't feed your children fast food and prepackaged snacks. They're high in sugar, sodium, fat and preservatives—and very low in nutrition. Why waste good money on empty calories? Give your kids a healthy head start in life by serving them fruits, vegetables and whole grains instead of burgers and fries. Opt for homemade trail mix and granola bars over potato chips and candy; and provide water as a beverage, rather than soda or sugary juice. These wholesome choices are not only cheaper than convenience foods; they reduce your child's risk of developing obesity, diabetes and other medical problems.

440 Pack your kids' lunches

Cafeteria food can be expensive—and hit-or-miss when it comes to nutrition. The frugillionaire solution: make your kids' lunches at home. Sandwiches, pasta salads, vegetables and fresh fruit are economical and healthy alternatives to standard school fare. Get your child on board with brown-bagging it, by making it a special treat: focus on their favorite foods, and ask for their suggestions. Cut food into cute shapes and bite-sized pieces to appeal to younger children; and pack extra snacks like pretzels, crackers and raisins to keep older ones away from vending machines.

441 Cut your kids' hair

The cost of kids' haircuts can really add up; skip the salon, and trim their locks at home! It's not rocket science, and requires little in terms of equipment. In most cases, a pair of hairdressing scissors will suffice; electric clippers are handy for boys with shorter cuts. Just remember to proceed slowly, and cut a little at a time; you can always take more off, but you can't put it back! Consult books on the subject for instruction, or watch video tutorials on the internet. At the very least, you'll learn to do some simple maintenance, and extend the time between professional visits.

442 Buy secondhand sports equipment

Outfitting kids for organized sports can be expensive—especially considering how fast they outgrow things! Shop at stores that specialize in secondhand sporting goods; you'll save money, and may even receive cash or credit for your used gear. You can also score some great bargains on Craigslist.com and eBay.com, and at thrift stores and garage sales. Alternatively, participate in a school- or community-sponsored "exchange day," an event during which outgrown sports equipment is traded among participants; skate swaps are particularly popular in youth hockey leagues.

443 Share chauffeur duties

Driving kids to school, ballet, soccer and piano lessons can make you feel like a part-time chauffeur; and filling the tank can be tough on your wallet! Save time and money by organizing a carpool with other parents in your area. Divide responsibilities by activity or day of the week, and maintain a regular schedule to avoid confusion. Make sure all parties have each other's cell phone numbers in case of emergencies or schedule changes. The more members in your carpool, the greater the savings; but even if you alternate with one other parent, you'll still cut your gas costs in half!

444 Be the teacher

Introducing kids to new activities is important to their development; but dance, karate and music classes can be expensive. Nurture their interests without going broke—by being the teacher! You'll find internet tutorials on almost any subject imaginable; pick up the basics, and pass them along to your children. Or join forces with a group of parents, and have each one teach a special "class"—like singing, baking or banging on the drums. That way, the kids can try a variety of hobbies, without the expense of a formal instructor. If your child shows promise in a certain pursuit, *then* consider paying for professional lessons.

445 Throw frugal birthday parties

Throw frugal—but fabulous—birthday parties! Good old fashioned fun doesn't have to cost a fortune. You'll score big savings if you skip the pricey venues, and hold the event in your own home or garden. To create a festive atmosphere, give the party a theme: like princesses, pirates, cowboys, animals, tropical island or outer space. Make your own decorations, and use your computer to design and print personalized invitations. Put together goodie bags with cookies, candy, and a small toy or favor you can buy in bulk. The kids will have a blast, and you'll stay on budget!

446 Raise little savers

Teach your children to save money at an early age, and you'll start them on the road to financial success. If you give them an allowance, or pay them for chores, show them how to save a portion of their earnings. Use a cute piggybank for little ones; when they're older, take them to the bank to open their very own savings accounts. Explain to them the difference between "wants" and "needs" so they'll understand how to make wise spending choices. Above all, set a good example: your kids should witness you depositing your paycheck and saving for purchases—rather than swiping your credit card and struggling to pay bills!

447 Limit advertising exposure

Children aren't born consumers; they're naturally content with what they have. So why all the screams and tears in the cereal aisle? Advertising. Eliminate this one element from their environment, and you'll have happier, healthier and more serene kids. Marketers know that children have a strong influence on their parents' purchases, so they bombard the tykes with ads from a very early age. Keep your kids out of their reach by turning off the television; encourage them to read, draw, or play outside instead. The fewer commercials they see, the less money it'll take to satisfy them!

448 Enlist your kids' help

Children may not have to work the farm anymore, but they can still pull their weight on the frugillionaire homestead! Ask older kids and teens to help with chores around the house, such as cooking, cleaning and babysitting younger siblings. They can also lend a hand with seasonal tasks—like mowing the lawn, raking leaves, or shoveling snow. Depending on your personal situation, you may or may not choose to compensate them with an allowance for their efforts. Either way, they'll learn valuable skills and a sense of responsibility; and you won't need to pay outside help for these services!

449 Take advantage of tax breaks

Don't forget your little darlings come April 15; they can earn you a hefty break on your taxes! Uncle Sam allows parents a variety of deductions and credits for their offspring. Most are based on income level, so cozy up with the tax code—or consult your accountant—to figure out what you qualify for. Potential breaks include child tax credits and exemptions; a dependent care credit for childcare expenses; an adoption credit; and deductions for college tuition and student loan interest. Higher-income taxpayers may benefit from Dependent Care Flexible Spending Accounts (DCFSAs), which allow parents to set aside pre-tax dollars to pay for childcare costs.

450 Consider a college savings plan

With tuitions on the rise, it's never too early to start saving for college! Consider enrolling in a state-sponsored "529" plan. Earnings in these accounts are free from federal income tax—and in many cases, state tax—as long as withdrawals are used for tuition, room and board, and other qualified higher education expenses. Consult a financial advisor to determine if a "529" plan is right for you. Assets in such plans can reduce financial aid eligibility, so you may want to accomplish other goals—such as paying off credit cards, purchasing a home, or saving for retirement—before contributing to one.

Chapter 13

HOLIDAY

Decking the Halls
without Going Into Debt

---

451 Give love from the kitchen

Everyone delights in a gift of baked goods! Whether it's brownies, cookies, cupcakes or breads, some love from your kitchen is sure to please. And best of all—it's budget-friendly! Making these delicious treats at home is significantly less expensive than buying them at the store. It's particularly cost-effective if you have a large gift list: you'll save money and time by buying ingredients, and baking, in bulk. Package them in low-cost tins, or paper plates wrapped with cellophane, and tie with a colorful bow for a festive touch. Recipients will remember your kindness, efforts and culinary prowess long into the future!

452 Give gifts in a jar

Homemade mixes in glass mason jars are a favorite frugillionaire gift idea. These creative concoctions provide the recipient with all the ingredients needed to whip up a tasty treat. Layer beans, lentils, dried vegetables and seasonings for a hearty soup mix; multi-colored noodles, herbs and spices for a pasta dish; flour, baking soda, sugar and chocolate chips for cookies; or cocoa, sugar, powdered milk and marshmallows for hot chocolate. Search cookbooks, or the internet, for plenty of ideas and recipes. To finish: top the jar with a seasonal fabric or ribbon, and affix a decorative label with cooking instructions.

453 Give an experience

Gifts can break, wear out or be tossed aside in a matter of months—or moments! The memories of a wonderful experience, on the other hand, can last forever. Think of something your recipient would love to *do*—rather than *have*—and arrange an activity that suits their interests. Take an artsy niece to a gallery opening, or a sports-nut nephew to a baseball game. Sign up a loved one for an introductory music lesson or cooking class. Treat a friend to a night at the theater. Experience gifts can be as frugal as they are fun: search around, and you'll find plenty of free activities, discounted tickets and low-cost classes to meet your needs.

454 Give your time

Give the gift of your time—it's more valuable (and will be more appreciated) than anything bought in a store! Offer to babysit for a friend's kids, so she and her husband can have a night out. Do household chores—like mowing the lawn, washing the windows, or making repairs—for elderly parents or relatives. Or share your skills and expertise: do someone's taxes, fix their computer, give them a massage, or teach them how to cook. For a formal flourish, present the recipient with a handmade coupon or certificate for your "services." A gift of your time costs you absolutely nothing; but to the giftee, it's priceless!

455 Give something small but decadent

Small indulgences make wonderful—and frugal—gifts! Choose an item the recipient would appreciate, but wouldn't splurge on herself. A small box of gourmet chocolates, jar of organic preserves, or bottle of high-end olive oil will delight a connoisseur without breaking the bank. Some decadent pastries from a local bakery are ideal for someone with a sweet tooth. Give a friend in need of pampering some bath salts, artisan soap or a luxurious hand cream. Focus on quality, not quantity—the smaller the amount, the more special it seems. Add some pretty packaging for an elegant touch!

456 Give something handmade

A handmade gift is much more special than a store-bought one—and your only cost is materials! Get creative: paint a picture, write a poem, or make your own ornaments. If you're handy with needle and thread, sew a pillow cover or cosmetic case. Or knit scarves, hats and mittens; they're winter holiday favorites that are especially cherished when made by a loved one. You can also purchase low-cost vases, bowls and boxes from craft stores and customize them with paint. Get the kids involved, too; it's a great holiday experience, and teaches them that the best gifts come from the heart!

457 Give photos

For a frugal, much-treasured gift—think family photographs! Find an old picture of your parents to commemorate their anniversary; gather childhood snaps of your sister to celebrate her 30th birthday; or give a friend a cute candid shot you recently took of her two-year-old. To accumulate material, tote along a camera to parties and family functions. Or reach out to relatives with old family photos, and offer to scan them into digital format. You'll not only preserve history, you'll build a wonderful image library for future gift-giving! To present the pictures: put single photos in frames, and multiples in mini-albums. Burn collections onto a CD or DVD for more tech-savvy recipients.

458 Give family heirlooms

Holidays, birthdays and special occasions are a great time to pass down family heirlooms. Not only does it save you from having to buy a gift; it's a chance to give sentimental pieces to those who will appreciate and enjoy them. In fact, the presentation of such a treasure—be it an old brooch, vase or set of china—often makes the occasion all the more special. Alternatively: if you've received such items, and they're not to your taste, consider gifting them to siblings or relatives who've admired them. You'll promote family harmony, save money, and declutter your house of unwanted possessions!

459 Give a beauty sampler

Cosmetic counters love to give out free samples—accept their generosity, and stash away these goodies for the holidays! Collect all the freebies you can, and make a beauty basket for someone on your gift list. Find a cute but inexpensive container, and fill it with all those high-end hand creams, eye shadows, lip balms and lotions you've accumulated over the year. Don't forget the mini-perfumes: gather them together into a little library of scents for a fragrance fanatic. Assembling such beauty samplers is a wonderful way to give high-end, luxury products—at little or no cost to you!

460 Give children the gift of financial security

Children enjoy simple pleasures, and don't require piles of presents to be happy. In fact, they often get more enjoyment from a gift's packaging than the item inside! Instead of spending all your money on things they'll quickly tire of, make an investment in their future. Buy just one or two special gifts, and contribute the rest of the budget to their college savings accounts. Encourage grandparents and relatives to do the same. The holidays will have a much more positive impact on their lives, providing them with a strong financial footing—rather than thousands of dollars worth of discarded toys!

461 Re-gift

When you receive a gift that's not to your taste, give it to somebody else! Re-gifting keeps perfectly good items out of the landfill, and perfectly good money in your pocket. Just follow a few simple rules when passing on your unwanted presents. First, make sure the item is appropriate for the recipient, and similar to what you would have bought them in a store. Second, re-gift outside the social circle (and preferably the region) of the original giver. And finally, don't re-gift something you've already used—send that gently-worn sweater to the thrift shop instead. If an item's too risky to re-gift: sell it on eBay.com, and use the proceeds to buy something new!

462 Create a holiday budget

Rein in holiday spending by setting a budget—and sticking to it! All too often, we use the "spirit" of the season as an excuse to splurge, and figure we'll worry about the bills the following year. Before the craziness starts, determine the dollar amount you can afford to spend *without going into debt*. Don't be afraid to set the bar low; frugillionaires can have wonderful holidays for under $100. List all expenditures (like gifts, decorations, food, parties and travel) and decide exactly how much you'll allot to each. When you have a plan, you're more mindful of your money—and more likely to save some of it for the New Year!

463 Buy gifts with cash

In the excitement of holiday shopping, it's easy to lose track of how much you're spending—especially when using a credit card. Swiping the plastic seems so painless, until the bills come due in January. Pay with cash instead, and you'll be acutely aware of every dollar you part with. To stick to your budget: fill an envelope with a predetermined amount, and make all purchases from this single stash. That way, you'll be forced to stop spending when the well runs dry. This system encourages careful planning and mindful shopping, and lets you start the New Year with financial peace of mind!

464 Make a gift list

Shop with a list—it's a powerful weapon against overspending. Before you even set foot in a store, outline all the people for whom you'll buy gifts, determine the amount you plan to spend, and decide exactly what you'll purchase for each person. Use the internet to brainstorm for ideas, check retailers' inventories, and find the lowest prices. When it's time to shop, buy what's on your list and nothing more. This deliberate, level-headed strategy not only keeps you on budget, it helps you give friends and family appropriate, thoughtful gifts—rather than whatever you could get your hands on in the last-minute rush!

465 Shop throughout the year

Save money, and your sanity, by purchasing gifts throughout the year—instead of at the last minute. The hectic pace of the holidays takes a toll on your wallet, as well as your nerves. When you're desperate for a gift, it's hard to be cost-conscious and consumer-savvy; you're more likely to overspend, just to get your shopping done. Instead, keep an eye out for gift-worthy items during the rest of the year, and buy them when they're on sale. Store them in a dedicated place (like a box, or closet shelf), so they're easily found come the holidays. This laid-back approach to gift shopping brings both serenity and savings!

466 Comparison shop online

If you're looking for a particular gift, go online to find the lowest price; it's faster and easier than driving all over town. With websites like PriceGrabber.com and mySimon.com, you can determine which store has the best deal in a matter of minutes. Search for a particular product, and the site lists all the retailers that have it in stock—along with their prices. Make the purchase online, with a few clicks of your mouse; or make note of the nearest brick-and-mortar outlet. You can even sign up to receive emails when the price of an item drops!

467 Have a gift exchange

Arrange a gift exchange, and give your holiday budget some breathing room! Buying presents for the whole family can quickly drain your bank account. Have everyone draw names instead, so that each person buys only one gift. Keep the results secret until the exchange; it's fun to speculate on "who has who," and adds extra excitement to your holiday shopping. Be sure to establish a spending limit to keep things in moderation. Try the same strategy with large groups of friends and coworkers. It'll save everyone a lot of time and stress, as well as money!

468 Set a spending limit

Gift giving on a budget doesn't have to be stressful; in fact, it can be great fun! Agree with family or friends on an arbitrary spending limit—such as $5, $10 or $25 per person. The lower the amount, the greater the challenge—and the more entertaining the results. You'll have plenty of laughs unwrapping a banana when your family has set a $1 budget! For the ultimate in frugality, try a "no-spend" holiday: gifts must come from personal possessions, or otherwise be made (or acquired) free of charge. You'll love the creativity it inspires, and the festive spirit that ensues!

469 Get everyone on board

Whether it's planning a gift exchange, setting a spending limit, or eliminating presents altogether, it's important to make sure that everyone's on board. Changing holiday traditions can be a sticky wicket; heed the following advice to smooth the process. First, present your proposal early in the year, before anyone has begun their shopping. Second, give it a positive spin: focus on fun as well as frugality, and emphasize the importance of spending time together over the exchange of gifts. And third, be willing to compromise; recognize that small changes in the right direction can ease your family into new, frugal traditions over time.

470 Cut down on the cards

Save money, and the environment, by cutting down on holiday cards—the vast majority wind up in the trash anyway! Start by paring down your list: send greetings only to those with whom you'd truly like to keep in touch. Consider a letter, or short phone call, instead—it's much more personal, and sure to be appreciated. For the cards you do send, try recycling the ones you receive; cut off the half with the image, and send as a postcard the following year. Or go virtual, and eliminate the cost of cards and postage altogether. Electronic greetings convey the same sentiments, without all the waste!

471 Reuse gift wrap

Don't send beautiful gift wrap to the landfill! Instead of tossing it in the trash, save it for future presents; simply wrap on a roll and secure with tape. Reusing wrapping paper—as well as ribbons, bows and other decorations—is good for both the environment and your budget. If you must purchase paper, choose solid colors (like silver, gold, blue or white) that work for a variety of occasions; or buy inexpensive brown kraft paper, and decorate with markers or stamps for a personal touch. Alternatively, wrap gifts with fabric; it looks gorgeous, and can be reused ad infinitum!

472 Hit post-season sales

Shop right *after* a holiday for the best deals on cards, wrapping and festive decorations. Nobody wants Halloween items on Nov. 1, Christmas ornaments on Dec. 26, or Valentines on Feb. 15—except frugillionaires! After a holiday, stores have leftover inventory and little demand, and mark down seasonal items dramatically to clear the shelves. Snap them up at deep discounts and store them away for next year. This simple strategy can save you as much as 75 to 90 percent over the retail price. Shop discriminately, though, and buy only what you truly need; no matter how low the price, useless clutter is never a bargain!

473 Decorate with nature

Skip the pricey, store-bought ornaments and decorate with nature instead! You don't have to spend a dime to deck the halls: simply look outside for items and inspiration. For example, gather pinecones to make a lovely centerpiece: pile them into a bowl, and spray with gold or silver paint for an elegant touch. Spread evergreen branches across your mantle, or spruce up your table with sprigs of holly. String popcorn and cranberries into garland for a festive yet frugal tree trimming. Using natural materials not only saves you money, it gives you greater appreciation for the beauty, and bounty, of the season!

474 Decorate with personal items

Let your seasonal décor reflect the true joy of the holidays: the chance to gather with, and appreciate, family! Decorate with items that have personal meaning, rather than expensive designer pedigrees: like heirloom ornaments, old photographs, and greeting cards from friends and relatives. They give a sense of warmth, tradition and meaning to your celebration. For a particularly delightful effect, ask children in the family to create special artwork for you to display. Their Santa drawings and paper chains are infinitely more charming than department store baubles!

475 Dress up generic décor

With a little creativity, you can give your house a holiday makeover without setting foot in the stores. Use the items you have on hand, and give them a fresh, seasonal touch. The same basket, for example, can hold Thanksgiving gourds, Christmas evergreens, or colorful Easter eggs; simply tie with a ribbon in an appropriate color. Use a similar method to dress up generic bowls and vases. Your money goes much further when you buy items that work for multiple occasions: like a simple white plate with a gold rim, instead of one emblazoned with reindeer and holly. It's not only economical—it's also more elegant!

476 Borrow items for entertaining

If you're entertaining a large group, but are low on hostess supplies—borrow them! Why blow your budget on extra items that'll only gather dust during the year? Your friends, family and neighbors are certain to have serving plates, silverware and folding chairs they'll be happy to lend. You may even be able to score some temporary table linens and seasonal decorations. Don't worry about mismatched plates or unusual utensils; an eclectic style sets an atmosphere that's fun and festive, rather than stuffy and formal. You can also augment your musical selection, by asking guests to bring their mp3 players or CDs!

477 Have a holiday potluck

The holidays are a perfect time for a potluck party! Ask attendees to bring their favorite seasonal dishes—such as childhood treats, secret family recipes, or traditional holiday foods from their cultural backgrounds. Have them write short explanations on place cards, to display alongside their contributions. Serve buffet style, so guests can mingle while they sample the offerings. Everyone will love the opportunity to expand their culinary horizons, and learn about each other's cultures and traditions. The best part: it'll hardly cost you a thing!

478 Celebrate simple pleasures

Celebrate the simple pleasures of the holiday season at home! Instead of going to the mall, gather your family around the hearth: cozy up in blankets, make hot cocoa and enjoy the flicker of a fire. Skip the movies (and other paid entertainment) in favor of old-fashioned traditions: like singing carols, roasting chestnuts, and reading classic holiday tales to the little ones. In our hectic lives, some seasonal activities—like baking cookies, wrapping gifts, and trimming the tree—can almost seem like chores. But if we slow down, and invite the whole family to participate, we can make them into fun—and frugal—holiday events.

479 Admire other people's décor

You don't need to cover your house with lights, or your lawn with reindeer, to get into the holiday spirit. Enjoy other people's décor instead! Make it a tradition to walk around your hometown, or drive to a neighboring one, to admire the seasonal decorations. Seek out particularly festive streets and decked-out homes for your outing; ask around your community, or check local papers, for prime locations. For an even more magical experience, visit a park or horticultural garden—many stage stunning holiday displays on a grand scale. It's much more fun than being up on a ladder, and you'll get all the enjoyment without the electric bills!

480 Join in community celebrations

The holiday season is the best time of year for free entertainment! Community celebrations offer plenty of frugal fun, as well as the chance to mingle with friends and neighbors. Attend the tree lighting in your town's main square at the start of the season. Then take your pick of the parades, parties, pageants and holiday concerts that follow. Check churches, synagogues and your local paper for event listings, and you'll never be at a loss for something to do. Not only are most festivities free, they're also family-friendly — providing wonderful opportunities to celebrate, and socialize, without the need of a sitter!

Chapter 14

PHILOSOPHY

Thinking Like
a Frugillionaire

---

481 Be a "minsumer"

Advertisers, economists and government officials define us as "consumers." They encourage us to buy as much as possible, so they can line their pockets, grow the GDP, and get re-elected. That may be good for corporations and politicians, but not our own bottom lines. Be a "minsumer" instead—acquire just enough goods to satisfy your needs, rather than shopping for its own sake. Minimize the role of consumption in your life, and make your mark on the world with your knowledge, creativity, and civic participation— rather than your purchases!

482 Focus on what you have

Take a few minutes and think about all the things you own; if you're feeling ambitious, get out pen and paper and make a list. It's a bit overwhelming, isn't it? Most of us have so much stuff, it seems ludicrous to feel any sense of deprivation. Yet marketers constantly turn our attention to what we *don't have*: things that we were perfectly content without before we saw their ads! Don't let them sway you into parting with your hard-earned cash. When you're tempted to buy something new, focus on what you already have. Heed the words of the *Tao Te Ching*: "If you realize that you have enough, you are truly rich."

483 Redefine success

We too often equate success with material accumulation, and feel we haven't "made it" until we own certain status symbols. So we set about acquiring them—credit cards in hand—and wreck our finances in the process. Follow the frugillionaire path instead, by redefining your concept of success. Forget the McMansions, sports cars and designer logos, and use your personal values to measure your achievement. Raising a happy family, excelling at your job, improving the lives of others, or living within your means are far better benchmarks of accomplishment!

484 Look down the ladder

Most of us fall somewhere in the middle of the economic continuum; there are plenty of people richer than us, and plenty of people poorer. If we're discontent, it's because we look only up the ladder, and compare ourselves to those who have more. For a balanced view, we must also look down—and see how some people struggle each day to survive. From this perspective, we gain a true picture of our prosperity. When we realize the privilege we have, we can turn our gaze from the higher rungs, and lend a hand to someone below. It costs a lot less than keeping up with the Joneses, and is infinitely more satisfying.

485 Lower your expectations

Expectations cause all sorts of trouble—as well as unnecessary expense! Imagine that your spouse gives you a diamond ring for your anniversary. If you hadn't anticipated such a gift, you'd be absolutely thrilled; but if you'd expected a stone twice the size, you'd spend the occasion down in the dumps. Expectations are the fine line between a happy and miserable life. When they're set too high—due to media, peers, or your own nature—you're sure to be disappointed. But when they're low (or nonexistent), life isn't nearly as tragic when things go awry—and all the more fabulous when they work out well!

486 Embrace the concept of "good enough"

Advertisers condition us to think we need the "best" of everything: the fastest car, the biggest house, the hippest clothes and the latest gadgets. Of course, these things usually come with the highest price tags! Instead of chasing superlatives, embrace the concept of "good enough." You don't need professional grade cookware to fix a nice meal, top-of-the-line speakers to groove to some tunes, or luxury sheets for a good night's sleep. Why pay for premium when "regular" will do? Be happy with what gets the job done, and save the "bigger and better" for your bank account!

487 Don't spend to impress

Money spent to impress others is usually money wasted. Realize that other people are too wrapped up in their own lives to notice—or care—if you have a professional pedicure, the latest designer outfit, or the cell phone du jour. Advertisers want us to think we live our lives in the spotlight; but in reality, very few of us are the objects of such rapt attention. Unless you're a celebrity, most people won't give a hoot about what you own or how you look. As for those who have nothing better to do than judge what *you're* wearing, driving or buying—they're hardly worth impressing!

488 Don't follow the herd

Fashion magazines and marketers tout the new "must-haves" every season—be it the "hot" handbag, skirt length, cell phone or mp3 player. They try to convince us that everyone else will be flaunting the latest, greatest and hippest stuff; and if we don't hurry up and buy, we'll be left behind. But chasing trends is a fool's game: in just a few months, that of-the-moment item will be yesterday's news. Instead of being a follower, be true to your own style. Buy things to satisfy needs, not for the sake of novelty. You'll save hundreds (maybe thousands!) of dollars each year—and a fat wallet is always in fashion!

489 Don't purchase a persona

We're all guilty of buying things for the life we wish we had, or the person we'd like to be. Maybe we have a closet of unworn evening gowns, a library of unread tomes, or a garage full of unused sports equipment. Somehow, purchasing those items didn't make us the socialite, scholar or sportsman we imagined! Shopping for a dream lifestyle is a waste of money; if your real life isn't glamorous, skip the bling. By the same token, don't let celebrities influence your consumption. What's appropriate for jet-setting actors may not be the best choice for you. Instead of imitating their style, celebrate your own!

490 Focus on appreciation, not deprivation

Marketers try to instill in us a sense of deprivation; they want us to feel empty and incomplete without the products they're selling. Become immune to their techniques by cultivating a strong sense of appreciation. When you're grateful for all the little things in life—a spring blossom, a loved one's smile, or the warmth of a fire on a winter night—you'll realize the abundance you already have. Take the time to cherish these moments, as they're far more valuable than manufactured goods. When a child's laughter or beautiful sunset makes your day, you'll feel wonderfully rich without spending a dime—and realize the true joy of being a frugillionaire!

491 Make do or do without

In some parts of the world, it's difficult to obtain basic goods, let alone anything considered "luxuries." People in such situations learn to make do with what they have—or simply do without. Be similarly resourceful when you feel the "need" to acquire a new possession. Consider if something you already own—perhaps altered, retooled, or re-purposed—can serve as a substitute. Alternatively, imagine how your life would be in the absence of this item: would it change for the worse, or simply go on as usual? If the latter, then do without—and save your money for more pressing needs.

492 Avoid advertising

Limit your exposure to advertising; you'll be amazed how carefree, happy—and rich—you become! When you don't know certain products exist, you don't want them. There's no reason to long for them, no pressure to buy them, and no stress to pay for them. Suddenly all these "problems" are eliminated from your life—it's incredibly liberating! Go on an advertising fast to see for yourself: cancel subscriptions to magazines, tune out television commercials, and install ad-blocking software in your internet browser. Saving is easier, and life more serene, when you're not bombarded with entreaties to "buy."

493 Give yourself some space

Less is more—these three words can change your life! Instead of filling your home with objects, and your time with activities, give yourself some space. You'll save money, and experience a wonderful sense of calm and serenity. Each extraneous thing you eliminate from your life—like an unused item, unnecessary purchase or unfulfilling task—feels like a weight lifted from your shoulders. You'll have fewer errands to run, and less stuff to shop for, pay for, clean, maintain and insure. When life is less cluttered with tchotchkes and to-do's, you have more time, money and energy to enjoy it!

494 Think before you spend

All too often, we let money slip through our fingers without a moment's thought—and then wonder where our paychecks have gone! From now on, carefully consider each purchase before whipping out your wallet. Ask yourself why you're buying a particular item: is it because it makes you feel sexy, because everyone else has one, or simply because you're bored? How many hours will you have to work to pay for it? Do you really need it, or can you live without it? When you question "why" before you buy, you'll increase your awareness—and decrease the amount—of your spending.

495 Live below your means

Spend less than you make, and your worries will be few! Banish the notion that you "deserve" a big house, new car or expensive clothes. Rather, be satisfied with the shelter, transport and raiment you can comfortably afford. Instead of taking on debt, find creative ways to meet your needs: get a roommate to help pay the rent; opt for the bus over an auto loan; shop secondhand rather than retail. Enjoy the challenge of saving as much of your paycheck as possible. And if your income increases, resist the urge to "upgrade" your lifestyle; keep your expenses low, and you'll be well on the road to riches!

496 Live simply

Mahatma Gandhi said, "Live simply so that others may simply live." Our planet's population is growing, and its resources are limited. When we over-consume, we take more than our fair share—leaving less for other people, and future generations. By limiting our personal consumption, we can avoid wasting the bounty of our earth on frivolous goods. We must also consider more than the price tag when making a purchase, and reject items made with exploited labor or ecologically harmful practices. No matter how cheap, it's not a bargain if another person—or our planet—is paying the price.

497 Less stuff equals less stress

Think of all the time and money usurped by a single possession. We plan for it, research it, and earn (or borrow) the money to buy it; purchase it, transport it home, and find a place to put it; maintain, insure, and clean it (or around it); and pay interest on it if we bought it on credit. We protect it from theft, fix it when it breaks, and pay someone to move it when we change abodes. Multiply that by a houseful of items, and it's exhausting just to consider! Take the easy way out, and buy less stuff: the fewer things you own, the less hassle and expense!

498 Less stuff equals more freedom

Possessions are like anchors. They tether us to our homes, because moving them makes it a hassle to relocate. They bind us to our jobs, because we must earn the money to pay for them. And they weigh on our souls, because even when we tire of them it's hard to throw them away. Avoid becoming a slave to stuff, by owning just enough to meet your needs. You'll not only gain financial freedom, you'll break the bonds of clutter. When you're not burdened with a pile of possessions—and the debt used to acquire them—you'll feel light, liberated and full of possibility!

499 Enjoy without owning

It's a joy to visit the Mona Lisa, but we wouldn't want to take her home. It would be quite a headache to keep her clean, secure and properly displayed—we'll leave that to the Louvre, thank you very much! Make your life easier (and less expensive) by finding similar ways to "enjoy without owning." For example, visit botanical gardens instead of planting exotics in your backyard. Swim in a community pool instead of maintaining your own. Rent a vacation home for a week instead of taking a mortgage on it. You'll often get *more* pleasure from things when you don't have the responsibility of ownership!

500 "Be" instead of "buy"

*You are **not** what you own*—remember these words whenever you feel the urge to splurge. Marketers try to make shopping an integral part of our lives; they encourage us to identify with the products we purchase, and shop as a means of self-expression. But when we become frugillionaires, a wonderful thing happens: we shift our focus from "buying" to "being." We break the spell of consumption and regain our freedom—from advertisers, from debt, and from the rat race. But more importantly, we redefine ourselves: by what we do, how we think, and who we love—rather than what we buy.

5649631R0

Made in the USA
Lexington, KY
01 June 2010